ISSUE 11, FEBRUARY 2021

AUSTRALIAN FOREIGN AFFAIRS

Contributors

Priya Chacko is a senior politics lecturer at the University of Adelaide and a fellow of the Australia-India Institute at the University of Melbourne.

Liam Cochrane teaches journalism at the University of Melbourne and was a South-East Asia correspondent for the ABC.

Melissa Conley Tyler is a research fellow in the Asia Institute at the University of Melbourne.

Kate Geraghty is a photojournalist for *The Sydney Morning Herald* and *The Age*, and a five-time Walkley winner.

Linda Jaivin is a novelist, essayist, translator and cultural commentator with a long-standing interest in China.

Natasha Kassam is a research fellow in the Lowy Institute's Public Opinion and Foreign Policy Program and a former diplomat.

John Keane is the professor of politics at the University of Sydney and the author of *The Life and Death of Democracy*.

Huong Le Thu is a senior analyst in the Australian Strategic Policy Institute's Defence and Strategy Program.

Darren Lim is a senior politics lecturer at the Australian National University and co-host of the *Australia in the World* podcast.

Sam Roggeveen is the director of the Lowy Institute's International Security Program.

Australian Foreign Affairs is published three times a year by Schwartz Books Pty Ltd. Publisher: Morry Schwartz. ISBN 978-1-76064-2105 ISSN 2208-5912 ALL RIGHTS RESERVED. No part of this publication may be reproduced, stored in a retrieval system, or transmitted in any form by any means, electronic, mechanical, photocopying, recording or otherwise, without the prior consent of the publishers. Essays, reviews and correspondence © retained by the authors. Subscriptions – 1 year print & digital auto-renew (3 issues): $49.99 within Australia incl. GST. 1 year print and digital subscription (3 issues): $59.99 within Australia incl. GST. 2 year print & digital (6 issues): $114.99 within Australia incl. GST. 1 year digital only auto-renew: $29.99. Payment may be made by MasterCard, Visa or Amex, or by cheque made out to Schwartz Books Pty Ltd. Payment includes postage and handling. To subscribe, fill out the form inside this issue, subscribe online at www.australianforeignaffairs.com, email subscribe@australianforeignaffairs.com or phone 1800 077 514 / 61 3 9486 0288. Correspondence should be addressed to: The Editor, Australian Foreign Affairs, Level 1, 221 Drummond Street, Carlton VIC 3053 Australia Phone: 61 3 9486 0288 / Fax: 61 3 9486 0244 Email: enquiries@australianforeignaffairs.com Editor: Jonathan Pearlman. Deputy Editor: Julia Carlomagno. Associate Editor: Chris Feik. Consulting Editor: Allan Gyngell. Digital Editor and Marketing: Amy Rudder. Editorial Intern: Lachlan McIntosh. Management: Elisabeth Young. Subscriptions: Iryna Byelyayeva. Publicity: Anna Lensky. Design: Peter Long. Production Coordination and Typesetting: Marilyn de Castro. Cover photograph by Feng Li / Getty. Printed in Australia by McPherson's Printing Group.

THE MARCH OF AUTOCRACY

In June 1987, a group of world leaders met in Venice to plan global economic policy for the twenty-first century. The leaders represented seven of the eight wealthiest countries in the world; the Soviet Union was excluded.

Addressing the summit, US president Ronald Reagan described the Soviet Union as an example of "how not to run a country". But he was less hostile towards China, which was then the world's ninth-largest economy, just ahead of Spain.

At the time, China's leader, Deng Xiaoping, was credited with overseeing a "second revolution" and introducing "sweeping economic reforms that have challenged Marxist orthodoxies" – as *Time* put it when naming him Person of the Year in 1985. If Deng's reforms work, the magazine predicted, "the world will not be the same".

In Venice, Reagan told his fellow democratic leaders that Deng's reforms marked "the first taste of freedom for over one billion people". Citing the spread of economic and political liberalisation across Asia,

Africa, and Central and South America, Reagan declared: "We look around the world and we see freedom is rising."

But that tide has turned. Today, autocracy, not democracy, is rising, and the new US president describes his Chinese counterpart as a "thug". Wealthy Western nations no longer confront a spluttering Soviet economy: the competition for global power and commerce is with China, the world's second-largest economy, on track to become the biggest by 2028. Of the globe's twenty wealthiest countries, China was the only one whose economy grew in 2020.

China's spectacular ascent has allowed its leaders to assert that one-party rule is crucial to its domestic growth and stability. "We considered them, tried them," said Xi Jinping in 2014, of political systems such as multi-party democracy, "but none worked."

Xi now confidently presents China as a model for others. The world's largest trading nation is partnering with other countries to develop ports, roads and infrastructure through its Belt and Road Initiative, and is planning to become a leading global technology supplier.

In recent years, as China has ascended, the United States and the European Union – the beacons of liberal democracy – have faltered. The global financial crisis of 2007–08 damaged Washington's global economic leadership. Its political divisions – culminating in the election of Donald Trump in 2016 and the breach of the Capitol in 2021 – damaged its global democratic leadership. The European Union has faced a debt crisis, a refugee crisis and, most recently, the departure of Britain, its second-wealthiest member.

There are now, for the first time since 2001, more autocratic states in the world than democracies. The 2020 annual report by Freedom House, a US government–funded organisation, found that 2019 marked the fourteenth consecutive year of decline in global freedom: "dictators are toiling to stamp out the last vestiges of domestic dissent and spread their harmful influence to new corners of the world", it said.

The COVID-19 pandemic – and Washington's and London's tragic mishandling of it – gave China an opportunity to promote the success of its heavy-handed governance model in suppressing the virus, even after it had tried to cover up the outbreak. Early last year, Serbia's president, Aleksandar Vučić, welcomed medical help from Beijing by kissing the Chinese flag and asserting that Serbians, no longer able to rely on the European Union for support, must instead depend on China. More recently, China has been distributing vaccines and promising access to countries including Indonesia, Malaysia, Thailand, Cambodia and Turkey.

For Australia, the world's autocratic turn has been confronting. Australia did not have a place at the Venice summit in 1987, but it did not need one. Instead, it viewed a US-led world order as best for its economic and security interests, and it tried to exercise international influence by remaining close to Washington.

The challenge for Canberra policymakers is not just that this old order is ending, but that the driving force behind the change is China, a country so crucial to Australia's future in Asia. Australia can and should resist the rising tide of authoritarianism, but it must also be aware of the consequences of doing so. Defending democracy, and condemning Chinese brutality and repressiveness in Xinjiang or Hong Kong, can carry a cost – as Australia's barley, beef and wine producers have learnt. Pushback against China and others should be careful and strategic. Australia needs a plan.

Beyond resistance, Australia must adapt. It needs to consider what a China-led globe will look like, the ways in which Beijing is likely to use its growing influence and how a country such as Australia can protect and promote its interests in a shifting world order. This does not mean appeasement, but recognising, understanding and adjusting to the new global reality.

Jonathan Pearlman

ENTER THE DRAGON

Decoding the new Chinese empire

John Keane

When future historians look back on our discordant times, they will surely note an epochal shift of global importance: the return of China, after nearly two centuries of humiliation, to world pre-eminence, and the bungled efforts to restore the American empire to greatness. But today this transformation comes wrapped in bitter disputes and conflicting predictions. Some policy specialists are sure that "the rise of China" is unsustainable, or that forecasts of its global triumph are grossly exaggerated. Others recommend getting tough with an uppity Beijing through trade wars and military clashes in the Taiwan Strait or in the South China Sea. Still others believe that a lengthy period of conflict – a new Cold War – is upon us, or that rough-tongued and cack-handed efforts to rejuvenate a militarily overstretched and fiscally overburdened America will have the unintended consequence of making China great again.

Like bellows to a fire, fallacies about China are inflaming controversies and stoking divisions. These misconceptions are dangerous because they spread confusion, attract simpletons, poison public life and blur political judgements. But which misconceptions are most urgently in need of correction?

The most obvious concerns the nature of the political system of the People's Republic of China (PRC). It is commonly said to be a worrying instance of "totalitarianism". But, strictly speaking, totalitarianism refers to a one-party political order ruled by violence, a single "glorious myth" ideology, all-purpose terror and compulsory mass rallies. The bulk of Chinese people would say that daily life in their country just isn't like that. The Mao days are over. There's a larger point here, for in reality China contradicts the key terms found in political science textbooks. The Chinese polity is something new. It's not a Mugabe-style corrupt military-bureaucratic dictatorship. It is neither an "autocracy" nor a "tyranny", if by those terms is meant a state ruled by a strongman consumed by lawless desires.

China watchers who tell us that Beijing's government is "totalitarian" or an "authoritarian dictatorship" or an "autocracy" sustained by the material benefits it delivers to its toad-eating subjects seriously misperceive things. Not only do they marshal Orientalist prejudices (kowtowing Chinese who haven't yet realised the beauty and benefits of Western liberal democracy), but they ignore the basic fact that citizens who stay inside the government's electric fences enjoy a wide range of daily freedoms without fear. In the PRC, state violence and repression are masked. Coercion is calibrated: cleverly camouflaged by elections, public forums, anticorruption agencies and other tools of government with a "democratic" feel.

Why do the Chinese Communist Party (CCP) leaders seek to win the loyalty of the population? The shortest answer: because they know the political dangers of self-aggrandisement. Their skittishness is palpable. From the Politburo Standing Committee all the way to the bottom, state officials know the teaching of ancient Chinese political thinkers: power does not in itself breed the authority required for enduring rule. The leadership instinctively grasps that jobs, full rice bowls, skyscrapers, shopping malls, and talk of socialism and holidays at home and abroad

Little sustains the political order beyond the population's loyalty

aren't enough to ensure their legitimacy. They know by heart the proverb that when trees fall, monkeys scatter. That's of course why the active public scrutiny and restraint of their arbitrary powers is both unwelcome and impermissible. They don't like open talk of China as a system of state capitalism that in the name of socialism hatches super-rich tycoons faster than any other country (257 billionaires in 2020 alone). The slightest whiff of a challenge to the CCP's power can bring down the hammer, as evidenced by mass detention camps in Xinjiang and crushed dissent in Hong Kong. But here's the thing: the rulers also know that rich and powerful people must fear too much power, just as pigs fear growing fat. They reject power-sharing, power-monitoring democracy, yet they fret about reckless abuses of power. That's why the CCP leadership trumpets China as a "people's democracy" and embraces a "phantom democracy" governing style (*shenjingshi min zhu*) that mocks but mirrors and mimics electoral democracies, where the fear of election defeat puts leaders in constant campaign mode.

Phantom democracy

What does it mean to call China a phantom democracy? Examples are plentiful. Most obvious is the proto-democratic style of the present leadership. In the hallowed name of the people, the Party showboats. It practises the common touch, as when President Xi – rumoured to be the world leader who's survived the most attempts on his life, but also has amassed more titles and formal powers than any Chinese leader since the 1940s, including Mao – springs a well-crafted "surprise" appearance and presses the flesh in a Beijing bun shop, rides a bicycle with his daughter, tips a humble trader in the back streets of Nanjing, praises state television journalists or kicks a Gaelic football during an official visit to Ireland.

Chinese phantom democracy extends well beyond leadership style. It includes village elections and the spread of "consultative democracy" into city administration and business. The telecommunications giant Huawei is an example: its governing board, called the Representatives Commission, comprises 115 employee representatives elected through secret ballot by the company's nearly 100,000 shareholder employees, who are scattered across more than 170 countries. Throughout China, state-funded "people's mediators" resolve conflicts, at no cost to litigants, in disputes over property and labour, divorce, and minor criminal and civil matters. There are neighbourhood assemblies, public hearings and experiments in participatory budgeting. Competition and "anti-corruption" mechanisms are built into state bureaucracies.

Chinese phantom democracy thrives on the clever use of digitally networked media as sophisticated tools to shape public opinion and policymaking, and as early warning devices. Yes, everybody knows the authorities censor and crack down on "inappropriate discussions". Dawn raids by plainclothes police, illegal detentions and violent beatings by unidentified thugs happen. Less well known is the way China's CCP rulers use digital media as a listening post – users are urged to vent their grievances, even to fight against the abuse of power. Since the early 1980s, the regime has built a giant information-gathering apparatus designed to shape public opinion. It has many parts, comprising hundreds of registered polling firms – including the Canton Public Opinion Research Centre (C-por), the largest such independent research agency in China, and the *People's Daily* Online Public Opinion Monitoring Centre, which uses data-harvesting algorithms to send summaries of internet chatter to officials in real time, often with advice about terms to use and avoid during public brouhahas. The apparatus also includes sophisticated digital strategies such as the Blue Map app, which informs citizens in real time about water quality and local sources of pollution; virtual petition sites, e-consultations and online Q&A sessions; and webcasts that come packaged in official assurances about the need to encourage transparency.

Underpinning these phantom democracy experiments is the idea that government stability rests on public opinion (*min yi*). Ignored by those who view China as a country run by totalitarian bullies and authoritarian autocrats, this principle is of utmost importance in grasping that the new Chinese despotism is equipped with shock absorbers, and therefore more resilient and durable than many suppose. When Xi Jinping told the Central Committee in 2013 that the survival of the regime depended on "winning or losing public support", he gave an old maxim a new twist. If opinion is the foundation of stable government, then the government must create stable opinion. In the name of "the people", the imperative is to keep an ear to the ground so that the goal of "guiding public opinion" towards harmonious rule becomes a reality. Cognisant of the errors of the Soviet Union, the party-state is aware it must consistently ensure the people's loyalty so that its "separation from the masses" never grows perilous.

In this way, oddly, the rulers of China acknowledge that power doesn't ultimately flow from the barrels of guns, or from Xinjiang-style interrogations, arrests and internments. They admit that little sustains the political order beyond the population's loyalty – their willingness to believe that the system addresses their complaints, and that democracy with Chinese characteristics is therefore better than its ailing "liberal" alternative.

A new Chinese empire

If the People's Republic of China is understood as a one-party phantom democracy, what can we to say about its burgeoning global role?

Here we encounter a second set of misconceptions. When Chinese intellectuals, journalists and diplomats are quizzed about China's foreign policy, they usually reply that the era of "crossing rivers by feeling for stones" (Deng Xiaoping) has been replaced by "crossings of oceans" (Xi Jinping). Scholars have told me that China's newfound global role is as a force for good, in harmony with the Confucian principle of "all under one heaven" (*tianxia*): China is becoming a great power (*daguo*), whose leaders have a responsibility to rule wisely over all in

> **China is an emergent empire of a kind never seen before**

their command. The inference is that China's leaders cannot be reckless: by stirring up political disorder or war, for instance, they would lose their "mandate of heaven" (*tian ming*). That is why, runs the reasoning, China wants to be a "humane authority to improve the world order", as Chinese public intellectual Yan Xuetong claims, and why it respects territorial sovereignty and doesn't interfere in the domestic affairs of others.

Note the absence of any mention of empire. In China, "empire" (*diguo*) is a pejorative term best directed at others. The historical fact that China was ruled by empires from the establishment of the Qin dynasty in 221 BCE to the fall of the Qing dynasty in 1911 is bracketed. State officials and media instead use the word to stress China's past victimhood ("the century of humiliation") at the hands of Western imperialism. In the United States, the word similarly triggers embarrassed silence. Americans regard themselves as a benign global power, upholding democracy and international cooperation. Former US secretary of defense Donald Rumsfeld said it clearly: "We don't seek empires. We're not imperialistic. We never have been." His words could just as easily have been spoken by the current Chinese leadership.

The Confucian edict that the beginning of wisdom is to call things by their proper name has clearly been scuttled. If by "empire" we mean a jumbo-sized state that exercises political, economic and symbolic power over millions of people, even at great distances from its own heartlands, without much regard for the niceties of territorial sovereignty, then technically China is already an empire. It's the word that's needed to describe accurately China's rising global role in such fields as finance capital, technology innovation, logistics, and diplomatic, military and cultural power.

China is an emergent empire of a kind never seen before. Let's call it a galaxy empire. The celestial simile helps describe a massive universe of institutions and activities gravitationally centred on the Beijing-led heartlands.

The most prominent project of this galaxy empire is the Belt and Road Initiative (BRI). Its scale and complexity are astonishing.

Launched in 2013, the huge program to build railways, roads, deep-sea ports, bridges, power grids and other infrastructure is set to cost more than a trillion dollars, seven times as much (when adjusted for inflation) as the United States invested in rebuilding Western Europe after World War II. Fifty special economic zones, modelled on the Shenzhen Special Economic Zone that Deng Xiaoping opened in 1980, are planned. When measured in terms of investment opportunities and export markets, and combined with domestic policies designed to boost income and consumption (such as Made in China 2025, which aims to turn China into a high-end producer of goods), it is clear that China's leaders are using BRI to craft an alternative to the US "pivot to Asia". For instance, the renminbi, China's official currency, is being promoted among BRI partners as a serious alternative to the greenback.

The BRI is funding megaprojects on a colossal scale: with plans to link more than sixty-five countries, there are currently 528 overseas projects with a contract value of over $50 million, and this figure is rising fast. Many of these projects – a $5.8-billion hydropower dam in Nigeria and a high-speed railway linking Kunming to Singapore, for instance – are still under construction, but the contours of the linkages are already clear. The original Silk Road of the Han dynasty period (206 BCE – 220 CE) powered an early wave of globalisation fuelled by trade networks that stretched west through central Asia, down to the Indian subcontinent and all the way to Europe. The BRI updates this expansionary vision. Beijing-financed infrastructure is reordering the lives of millions, from South Africa, Nigeria, Hungary, Greece, Iran and Sri Lanka to Cambodia, Papua New Guinea, Jamaica, Mexico and Argentina. Every continent is touched by the new empire, including Antarctica, where China will soon open its fifth polar station, and is out-investing the United States and Australia in research and development.

None of this should surprise. China has already surpassed the United States as the world's largest trading nation. It holds half the globe's patents and has outflanked bodies such as the International Monetary Fund and the World Bank to become the planet's largest creditor. It's now Africa's biggest trading partner, and rivals the United States in Latin America, where Chinese investment, extraction of resources and trade jumped tenfold in the first decade of this century, with China now the largest buyer of iron, copper, oil and soybeans in the region. It's clear as well that the great pestilence currently disrupting the world is working to China's advantage. In 2020, the country accounted for an unprecedented 30 per cent of global economic growth. Despite facing a rapidly ageing population, China appears to be succeeding in its determination to escape the so-called middle-income trap (the failure to shift from low-skilled manufacturing to higher-value goods and services) that during the past generation bedevilled close to 90 per cent of countries that reached China's level of wealth.

What is the long-term significance of these trends? What kind of Chinese empire is emerging at the global level?

The new Chinese empire already defies some classic distinctions. European empires depended on a capitol and key cities in their colonies. China, by contrast, is preoccupied with capital of a different sort: the flow of investment, the spread of networked information technologies and the growth of global markets for its competitively priced goods and services. It connects cities and hinterlands by high-speed railways, airports and shipping lanes. Buoyed by its dependence on digital communication networks, fluid mobility is its currency.

Britannia could not have ruled the waves without coal-fired steam engines and sails. The railroad and telegraph enabled the young American empire to push westwards. The vast global reach of China is strengthened not by clippers and copper wire but by networked communications systems backed by giant state-protected corporations – such as the ecommerce and technology behemoth Alibaba, and Tencent, the controller of the multipurpose messaging app WeChat, used by 1.2 billion people worldwide. These companies are key stakeholders in the "cyber-sovereignty" net China is casting over spaces well beyond its borders. This model, a serious rival to Silicon Valley, promotes high-speed broadband flows of information in support of China's governance, investment and financing schemes, and ideas, news and culture. The empire's surging foreign press corps is an example. Journalists at

[China is] an information empire, propelled by commercial interests

the China Global Television Network and the *China Daily* newspaper are more than reporters filing stories from abroad; they double as intelligence providers for the party-state. And cyber-sovereignty is big business. The empire sells its techniques and tools, as in South Africa, the first African country to buy a Huawei-powered 5G network to support smart healthcare, ports, mining and manufacturing.

Harold Innis's much-vaunted distinction between militaristic empires fixated on space and religious empires preoccupied with time is not meaningful with China. It's not a gunpowder or dreadnought battleship or B-52 bomber empire. It's an information empire, propelled by commercial interests, innovations such as the Beidou ("Big Dipper") global satellite navigation system and multipolar governing arrangements.

Striking is the degree to which China has committed to participating in and building cross-border institutions. Declining empires talk big but look inwards, retreating to strongholds and building walls. Rising empires look towards horizons and fling themselves into – and onto – the world. Through institutions such as the Shanghai Cooperation Organisation alliance and the Chiang Mai Initiative currency-swap arrangement, China actively partners with its fourteen neighbouring states. It plays a high-profile role in regional bodies such as the Asia-Pacific Economic Cooperation (APEC) and the Regional Comprehensive Economic Partnership. Institutional restructuring and the soliciting of leadership roles within global bodies is equally high on its agenda. China already heads four of the fifteen United Nations agencies. In recent years, it has helped build, and now leads, multilateral institutions such as the China-Arab States Cooperation Forum, which are founded on pragmatic consent, not formal treaty alliances.

Kaleidoscopic government

How does China behave within these institutions? Here's another novelty: this empire isn't framed by a dominant ideology. Empires of old typically ruled through a set of legitimating symbols – the Portuguese and Spanish emperors were proselytes for monarchy and the church. China critics say its rulers are in the grip of Marxist–Leninist ideology, while scholars such as Rana Mitter worry about a "new nationalism". But both assessments miss the point that at home and abroad the regime's leaders come dressed in colourful coats made of different languages and styles. They take a leaf from the book of Charles V, the legendary sixteenth-century Holy Roman Emperor who learned so many languages to help him rule over his vast empire that he was said to speak Spanish to God, Italian to friends, German to enemies and French to lovers.

The promoters of China's galaxy empire speak in tongues. This gives them the tactical advantage of sailing with the political winds and being different things to different people in different times and places. They are hard to pin down. The worship of country means that state-enforced amnesia about past mistakes is compulsory – an obligation acclaimed Chinese author Ma Jian satirises in his novel *China Dream* with "China Dream Soup", a broth of eternal forgetting.

But what's equally significant is the way CCP leaders spout mantras such as "socialism", "harmonious society", "people's democracy", "rule of law", "ecological civilisation" and "ancient Chinese civilisation". Government, business and cultural leaders all adopt this rhetoric when operating abroad. Power craves authority, which is why the empire throws its cultural weight around on the global stage. Mercedes-Benz was humbled into apologising for Instagramming an inspirational quote from the Dalai Lama. Foreign airlines were pressured into deleting online references to Taiwan. The Houston Rockets basketball team paid dearly for its general manager's tweet in support of Hong Kong protesters.

But there's evidence that China's officials and their media publicists are conscious of the reputational dangers of ideological attacks on free expression. They know those who grow thorns reap wounds, and that's why they want to be seen as champions of peace and tolerance, wealth creation and good governance. Within bodies such as the World Trade Organization, Chinese diplomats and negotiators display strong commitments to rule-of-law precepts and often impress outsiders with their knowledge of procedural rules and technical details, their preparedness and their tough negotiating skills. In matters of public image, there are paradoxical moments, as when the Chinese government – the enemy of multi-party elections – out-flanked the European Union and the United States by providing Cambodia with computers, printers, voting booths, ballot boxes and election monitors in support of its sham mid-2018 general election;

and when China donated large quantities of personal protective equipment to Myanmar, to be used in its 2020 general election.

The de-facto emperor displays a similar kaleidoscopic style. Xi Jinping, the "Chairman of Everything", doesn't exude the unchecked megalomania of dictators such as Napoleon, Stalin and Hitler. He's more like Shakespeare's Duke of Gloucester, confident in his ability to boost the power and prestige of the empire by adding colours to a chameleon and changing shapes with Proteus. He gives a whole new meaning to dialectics: at home, he's a tough-minded, iron-fisted champion of "socialism", head of the armed forces and benevolent man of the people; abroad, he dons the mantle of moral redeemer, champion of ancient Chinese civilisation and stout defender of peace through multilateral institutions.

Predictions of China's future are warped by wishful thinking

China's leaders are acutely aware of the pitfalls of military over-stretch. That's why they seek to calm nerves by promoting their empire as a force for peace. This portrayal rests upon spin, silence and secrecy: according to Stockholm International Peace Research Institute (SIPRI) data, for instance, China is now the second-largest arms manufacturer, behind only the United States, and it has more cruise missiles and middle-range ballistic rockets than its great-power counterpart. The PLA's navy is the world's largest. Military bases to supplement its existing Djibouti and Tajikistan installations are no doubt in planning.

China's public relations task is nevertheless made easier by the fact they are up against an American empire that some would say is obscenely overarmed. Those who speak of China as a "bully" and an "aggressor" must remember that the United States remains the world's commander-in-chief. It has military bases and installations in 150 countries, and according to SIPRI spends more on its armed forces than the next ten countries combined.

China's reputation as an irenic empire is reinforced by active contributions to United Nations peacekeeping operations – for instance, clearing landmines on the southern Lebanon border with Israel. Its best-known foreign engagements so far have been *withdrawals* of Chinese civilians from conflict zones, as in Libya (2011) and Yemen (2015), where a Chinese version of the "responsibility to protect" ("military officers must be the guardians of the people's security, and military ships must be like Noah's Ark for our compatriots" was the foreign ministry spin) suddenly replaced the doctrine of non-interference in the affairs of other states. Finally, its claim to be a force for peace is bolstered by its unconventional military strategy towards the United States: since it is not an empire in a hurry, it can act under Sun Tzu's guidance to wear down its competitor by avoiding war, demonstrating that deferral and avoiding "lengthy operations in the field" can yield lasting victories.

The next imperial age

The history of empires is suffused with talk of "decline", "fall" and "collapse" for good reason. Even the mightiest empires are eventually undone by their excesses – by rising costs and revenue shortages, by corruption and cumbrous administration, by unrest on their margins.

Opinions about the sustainability of the new Chinese empire are divided. Former US secretary of state Henry Kissinger is among those who are convinced that we have entered the Chinese Century. Others say the growth dynamics can't last, that Xi Jinping's galaxy empire will suffer the fate of many of China's past dynasties. Who is right? What can we say about the durability of the new galaxy empire?

Here there's a third cluster of misconceptions. Predictions of China's future are warped by wishful thinking. "I'd give the regime a couple of years, no more than a decade," a prominent China scholar told me three years ago. He's been saying that for three decades. The bravado is the flipside of the ill-fated 1990s prediction that market reforms would turn China into an American-style liberal democracy. Regime collapse is also on the political agenda of hawks, who liken China to a house of cards, liable to be scattered by a firm flick of the wrist. They want a new Cold War. They're convinced of the moral superiority of American democracy. They regard China as a dragon power responsible for the theft of American jobs and a global pestilence. Like former Trump adviser Stephen K. Bannon, they are sure that "the lies, the infiltration and the malevolence" of its rulers render China just as vulnerable to collapse as its Soviet predecessor.

They stir up public sentiment against the "totalitarianism" and "authoritarianism" of the CCP-led regime. They see acts of silent espionage and systematic takeovers of businesses, governments, universities, newspapers, churches and civil society bodies beyond China's borders. They warn of threats to "sovereignty" and the coming death of liberal democracy.

There is some validity in these warnings. Empires always try to shift the balance of power to their favour. The trouble is this new Cold War politics spreads fickle misconceptions. It understates the resilience of the phantom democracy that anchors the CCP regime. The warriors' sense of the history of empires, masterfully probed in such works as John Darwin's *After Tamerlane* (2007), is feeble. They wrongly imagine the new Chinese empire to be a repeat of Ottoman bribery, corruption, decadence and quarrelling advisers. Talk of "getting tough with China" functions as a call to discomfit and debase China – it is a cry of pain from within "the West". It attracts xenophobes, racists and Orientalists. These bull-in-a-China-shop warriors seem blasé about the probable consequences of the desired downfall – "the collapse of a world empire," notes the German scholar Herfried Münkler, "usually means the end of the world economy associated with it." They may be picking a fight that delivers political, economic and reputational setbacks to the United States, or further hastens its demise as an imperial power.

Reckless China-bashing and moonstruck love affairs with America are dead ends. Talking up military aggression in the age of nuclear weapons is madness. Since there is no Thucydides Trap (the idea that armed conflict is almost inevitable when a rising empire challenges an established one), except in the heads of the New Cold Warriors, a realistic strategy for dealing with China is needed.

We could call it agile non-alignment. Governments, businesses, non-government organisations and citizens committed to engaging critically with China would embrace cooperation in such fields as infrastructure development, scientific research, higher education and renewable energy. Some prickly exchanges with Chinese partners would be expected. Former Australian prime minister Kevin Rudd was on to something: when it comes to dealing with China and its allies and opponents, he

> **[China's] leaders are already being reminded that resistance and social unrest are the price of influence and control**

liked to say, truly durable friendships (*zheng you*) are built on unflinching advice and frank awareness of basic interests and ambitions. Such frankness can yield positive results. On this logic, breaking up with China isn't necessary. It would be self-destructive and foolish.

Agile non-alignment would necessitate the opening of minds: a new willingness among political thinkers, journalists, citizens and politicians to dissect their own ignorance about China, to see with fresh eyes its complexity and to avoid underestimating its shapeshifting resilience. The evidence speaks against the exaggerations of those, like the global China editor of the *Financial Times*, who claim that "the wheels are falling off the BRI" and "fiascos are piling up"; that a China "so vaunted for planning its own extraordinary development" is being revealed as "largely unable to pull off the same feat abroad". Such generalities not only downplay the CCP's crisis management capacities, demonstrated yet again by its handling of the COVID-19 pestilence it hatched. They underplay the empire's structural weaknesses.

Imperial flaws, democratic openings

What are the faults and flaws of the new Chinese empire? Most obviously, it is dogged by legitimacy problems. Its leaders are already being reminded that resistance and social unrest are the price of influence and control. They are learning that they cannot unilaterally determine the habits and hopes of people who fall within the ambit of the empire by using methods trialled in Tibet, Xinjiang and Hong Kong.

Every Chinese government official, diplomat and businessperson should read *The Vizier's Elephant* (1947) by Nobel Prize winner Ivo Andrić, the classic tale of resentment against the pinched promises and hypocrisy of occupiers, to grasp how easily imperial power can be doubted, satirised, worn down and defeated. The age of communicative abundance makes cultural resistance – mutinies against the maltreatment of local workers, for instance – much easier. Digital tools give new life to the Chinese writer Lu Xun's principle that "discontent is the wheel that moves people forward". Local disenchantment with the empire can readily follow – as happened, for instance, in Kazakhstan in 2019, with large-scale protests against the construction of Chinese factories and the maltreatment of Muslim and Turkic peoples in Xinjiang; and in Zambia, where bitter clashes between local mining workers and their Chinese employers have been rife for decades.

There's also a flaw that troubles all empires: chronic tensions between the central rulers and administrators at the periphery. The Dutch East India Company was constantly troubled by disputes with distant ship captains, company representatives and local governors. British mishandling of its American colonies ended badly. China's difficulties in Libya in 2011 provided a similar lesson: when state-owned companies invested in the local petroleum industry and infrastructure projects, they never anticipated that the collapse of the Libyan regime would require a military rescue operation that inadvertently publicised suspected Chinese arms sales to the Gaddafi regime and embarrassed the Ministry of Foreign Affairs. The galaxy empire stumbled. Talk of "non-interference" in "sovereign" states was dropped. After declining to veto a UN Security Council resolution sanctioning NATO bombing of Gaddafi's forces, China then urged compromise with the regime and condemned the air strikes. As the regime collapsed, Chinese forces intervened to protect seventy-five Chinese companies and deliver 38,000 workers to safety.

In the coming years, legitimacy problems and tensions between centre and periphery are bound to trouble the Chinese empire, exacerbated by local and regional concerns about how mounting debt conflicts are to be handled – by persuasion, legal proceedings or force.

There are environmental concerns, too. China invests much more in renewable energy than the United States, yet at least a third of its groundwater is unfit for human consumption. And there are bio-challenges abroad, in places such as Antarctica, where the Chinese-owned Shanghai Chonghe Marine Industry Company, awaiting delivery of the world's largest krill-fishing boat, is sure to encounter protests against its profit-driven plans to mega-harvest the small crustacean currently suffering population decline in delicately balanced biomes.

These vulnerabilities feed China's greatest flaw: its lukewarm and contradictory embrace of public accountability mechanisms. China's leaders say they want open connectivity and uncorrupted cross-border institutions based on consultation. Yet, as a one-party regime, it requires secrecy, dissimulation and unchallenged power. Several leading Chinese international relations scholars have told me privately that their country can't succeed globally unless it opens its power structures to much greater scrutiny, both at home and abroad. Its currency must be eternal vigilance, wise deference to complexity, humble open-mindedness. They have a point: the fundamental weakness of every expanding empire is bombast and vulnerability to public exposure and public rejection. This weakness is especially threatening to an empire born within the information age. Put bluntly, democracy shortages are China's greatest weakness.

Well-functioning monitory democracies nurture watchdog bodies such as public enquiries, judicial review and futures commissions that serve as risk-reduction mechanisms, designed to deal with threatening uncertainties, corruption and nasty surprises. At home and abroad, China tries to mimic these methods. In places such as Sri Lanka, poster campaigns announce the coming of "extensive consultation, joint contributions, shared benefits". Yet unexpected events can extinguish these promises. A corruption scandal, poisoned food chains, the collapse of a corporate behemoth or sudden social resistance to infrastructure projects can rock China's power to its foundations. Small beginnings can hatch big dramas. Democratic openings can occur. Backed by demands

It may be that China ... develops a commanding resilience

for public accountability, supported by civil society organisations and political leaders, the push for monitory democracy can spread – even across borders, into the heartlands of the empire. Cross-strait troubles with democratic Taiwan might well prove to be an example in the coming months and years.

But it may be that China's galaxy empire develops a commanding resilience most observers hadn't anticipated. Among the biggest imaginable surprises might be that its rulers, tempered by skittishness and smart governing methods, succeed not only in harnessing phantom democratic mechanisms at home to legitimate and strengthen their single-party rule, but also abroad, in the far-flung districts of their empire. China might perfect the art of what has been called "administrative absorption": the ability to win over resistance, to convince clients everywhere that Chinese infrastructure projects, ways of life and commitments to multilateral governance are universally good, and clearly superior to the confused American alternatives on offer.

Suppose the present Chinese political system stays on track to humble the United States. That its economy becomes twice as large, with its well-educated population at least half as wealthy as Americans. Then imagine that those who govern the new Chinese empire outdo the Ottomans and the British by cleverly paying homage to their subjects everywhere, employing surprising degrees of self-scrutiny, experimentation and administrative absorption. Let's further imagine that a mix of economic growth, social policy, state surveillance, political repression, middle-class support, dreams of restoring China to greatness and American foolishness all help to fertilise its power. Wouldn't China become the global torchbearer for one-party government grounded in the willing loyalty of its people – a strange new post-democratic regime with a democratic feel? Not a "thoroughgoing return to totalitarian politics", as Chinese scholar Xu Zhangrun has warned, but a tremendously powerful phantom democracy triumphantly beating a path towards a world with little or no room for the power-sharing constitutional democracy of earlier, happier times. ■

FUTURE SHOCK

How to prepare for a China-led world

Natasha Kassam
& Darren Lim

It is the year 2049. China is celebrating having reached its second centenary goal – to become a "prosperous, powerful, democratic, civilised and harmonious socialist modernised country" by the 100th anniversary of the People's Republic. Its economy is three times the size of the United States', as the International Monetary Fund predicted back in the 2010s. The United States remains wealthy and powerful – it has functioning alliances in Europe – but its pacts with Asian allies, almost a century old, have fallen into disrepair.

For decades, Hong Kong has been accepted as just another province of China. Few dare to criticise the ongoing human rights abuses there, or in Xinjiang and elsewhere, because of the extraterritorial application of China's national security laws. Taiwan, if not annexed, is isolated, with no diplomatic partners. The legacy of Xi Jinping, who led China for more than thirty years, monopolises ideological discourse in China, and his successors rule under his shadow.

Outside China, many of the third-wave democracies that transitioned in the second half of the twentieth century have become far less liberal. Elections are held, but increasingly authoritarian governments have adopted many of Beijing's technological and legal tools to manage markets and control politics. The internet is heavily censored. Stability, development and "harmony" eclipse the rights of the individual in much of the world.

Very little light gets through the digital iron curtain. Mistrust permeates every aspect of China's relations with the West. International cooperation on climate change and the strong carbon reduction commitments of the early 2020s have long been abandoned, and the focus is on individual adaptation.

Australia remains a liberal democracy, and a staunch defender of free markets and human rights. But these are no longer the default standards of global governance – they are minority positions associated mostly with Western traditions. No longer a top-twenty economic or military power, Australia's opportunities to make its mark internationally are few and far between.

This vision of a fragmented and decidedly less liberal international order is highly speculative, but also dispiritingly plausible. It is unsettling to an Australian reader, not just because Australian foreign policy has been centred on a global set of rules and institutions since 1945, but because Australian identity is so enmeshed with the values of liberal democracy. The 2017 Foreign Policy White Paper states that

Canberra is "a determined advocate of liberal institutions, universal values and human rights", in stark contrast to Beijing.

All nation states, especially rising powers, desire a favourable global environment in which they can acquire power, prosperity and prestige. The postwar system greatly aided China, and it would be incorrect to claim that Beijing wants to dismantle it entirely. Similarly, it would be disingenuous to overlook the many instances where the United States and other liberal democracies have behaved inconsistently. In particular, Washington has abused the privileges of its hegemonic status, allowing hubris and narrow self-interest to eclipse broader principle, feeding a crisis of legitimacy that would exist regardless of China's rise.

The rising tide of development has played into the CCP's ideological narrative

But the Chinese Communist Party, which leads an authoritarian one-party state, sees the liberal values embedded in the present order as a threat to its rule. Unlike the United States, which at times ignores or violates these principles, China needs many of them to be suppressed, even eliminated. As China seeks to remake the international order, the challenge is to understand where and how Beijing's efforts will undercut its liberal character, and to identify where it is possible to resist.

All politics is local: the China model

In today's China, the policies that emerge from the halls of Zhong-nanhai all have a central tenet: regime survival.

Yet no political system – even those that do not involve elections – can survive indefinitely without a degree of popular support. The CCP must blend a positive vision that promotes its legitimacy with hard-nosed enforcement to eliminate real and perceived threats. The result is a unique political and economic system – the "China model" – designed to sustain China's rise while keeping the Party in power.

China's leaders use the concept of "rejuvenation" – the commitment to rebuilding a strong, stable, wealthy and confident nation – to reinforce their legitimacy. Rejuvenation requires economic prosperity and political stability, but also links to specific narratives and ideologies. These include celebrating the CCP's own "long march" to power under Mao, Marxism–Leninism and the glories of China's historical past, and invoking the century of humiliation. These narratives cast the Party as indispensable to the modern China project – "ideological security" is central to China's political model. Party-approved speech, including the slavish celebration of Xi in state media, drowns out other voices.

The darker side of Chinese authoritarianism eliminates threats to the CCP's legitimacy. For most Chinese citizens, this manifests as an officious bureaucracy, mass surveillance and internet censorship, which they tolerate or accept. But for ethnic minorities, religious groups, journalists, lawyers and other persecuted groups, the consequences are severe. For example, the litany of human rights violations against Uighurs in recent years, including mass internment, are well documented. Individuals and groups critical of the Party suffer political purges, arbitrary detention, disappearance and forced confessions.

Since the Tiananmen massacre in 1989, the rising tide of development has played into the CCP's ideological narrative, proving sufficient to sustain its legitimacy. China's economy has thrived. Export-oriented and investment-led state capitalism has created an economic powerhouse, and hundreds of millions of Chinese people have lifted themselves out of poverty.

China capitalised on that growth, leveraging the international system to accumulate prosperity and prestige. It became a great power and emerged as a rival to the United States. At the same time, the West's strategy of engagement minimised external threats to the CCP's survival, while providing the economic opportunities to turbocharge China's development.

But sustaining the Party's legitimacy is becoming an increasing challenge.

Today these favourable conditions are gone, in many ways a victim of China's success. Economic growth has slowed, requiring painful reforms, and the country faces major demographic and environmental challenges. If the declining birth rate continues, China's population could decrease by more than half by century's end, and in 2050 pension spending will drain over 20 per cent of government spending, up from 3 per cent in 2016. Xi describes these challenges as the new "principal contradiction" facing China. No longer is the schism between "the ever-growing material and cultural needs of the people and backward social production", as Deng Xiaoping announced in 1981, but between "unbalanced and inadequate development and the people's ever-growing needs for a better life".

As the foundations of the domestic "rejuvenation" narrative weaken, the solution to this principal contradiction increasingly has an international dimension. The world stage offers opportunities for the CCP to boost its credibility as the architect of China's return to greatness. However, this opportunity has trade-offs. China's expanding interests are resulting in clashes with others. Growing power is meeting growing resistance.

Taking the China model global

International orders reflect the character of the great powers that found and lead them. The postwar "liberal international" order reflected the United States' own liberal democracy, not just its hard-headed interests. Washington's leadership was based on its military and political power (and the privileges this afforded), but also on an open and reciprocity-based system of rules, institutions and norms.

Domestically, the China model delivers material success while preserving the authority and legitimacy of the CCP. In the Party vision, a China-led international order would follow a similar logic. China needs a system that promotes rejuvenation, without undermining the ideological security of CCP rule.

The problem is that the pursuit of rejuvenation and ideological security are in contradiction. In a modern, globalised world, rejuvenation requires engagement beyond Beijing's borders. China needs its students to travel overseas and study at the best institutions to bring home world-standard skills and knowledge. It needs its companies to learn from major multinationals to seek to compete with them. It needs its diplomats to build cooperative relationships with other governments in order to navigate the multilateral system and to solve global problems such as pandemics and climate change. But engagement threatens ideological security. Exposing China and its people to a liberal world order that elevates human rights and a robust civil society, an impartial

The twentieth-century authoritarian playbook is no longer effective

rule of law, and democratic transparency and accountability serves to highlight the absence of these features in its system.

For China's leaders, the collapse of the Soviet Union is a constant reminder of the need to remain focused on Party legitimacy, no matter the incentives to engage with the outside world. In 2013, a Chinese military university made an educational film cautioning that the Soviet Union, under relentless US pressure, "gave up its political banner, gave up its ideals, gave up its ideology, stopped watching its enemy and eventually confused itself". The warning was clear: the United States would target China next. The Soviet Union's collapse is only more instructive because of its economic stagnation, which is one of the motivations behind Xi's reforms in finance and macroeconomics.

A leaked Party directive from April 2013 makes some of these fears of the US-led order clear. It condemns those who "use Western constitutional democracy to undermine the Party's leadership" and deems "universal values", "civil society" and "freedom of the press" as threats, concluding "we must reinforce our management of all types and levels of propaganda on the cultural front ... and allow absolutely no opportunity or outlets for incorrect thinking or viewpoints to spread".

Along with aggressively quashing threats to ideological security at home, the Chinese government has built barriers, real and virtual, to prevent liberalism from crossing its borders. But in an era of unprecedented interdependence between states, and digitally connected citizens within them, the twentieth-century authoritarian playbook is no longer effective.

Internationally, the CCP wants to silence criticism of its rejection of liberal ideas and to be actively celebrated for its economic successes and social stability. China's leaders are aware that countries which respect and want to emulate the China model will be willing partners in Beijing's efforts to reshape the system. Their compliance, and praise of the China model, offer propaganda value at home.

All rising powers, indeed all states, aspire to increase their global influence. But the Party's ideological security demands more – not just an international system where the China model can exist, but one in which it serves as an example for other countries.

The Party makes no secret of these goals. Here is Xi at the 19th Party Congress in 2017:

[T]he banner of socialism with Chinese characteristics is now fly-ing high and proud for all to see. It means that the path, the theory, the system and the culture of socialism with Chinese characteris-tics have kept developing, blazing a new trail for other developing countries to achieve modernization … It offers Chinese wisdom and a Chinese approach to solving the problems facing mankind.

How China changes the world

Rather than upend the existing international system, Beijing's approach today is to co-opt, ignore and exploit institutions selectively. Xi has said that "reforming and improving the current international system do not mean completely replacing it, but rather advancing it in a direction that is more just and reasonable".

In late 2019, for instance, the World Trade Organization's Appellate Body ceased to function after the United States – complaining about the organisation's soft stance on China – blocked the appointment of replacement judges. In many ways, the WTO's structure is the epitome of a liberal rules-based system: countries relinquish some sovereignty and are bound by judicial decisions in the interests of resolving trade disputes. In response, China joined with the European Union, Australia and other governments to set up a parallel stop-gap legal mechanism. This was a reflection of the CCP's nuanced relationship with the liberal international order. China needs a stable trading system and will agree to binding rules to preserve it. The odd trade dispute does not substantially threaten China's ideological security.

In the future, Beijing should be expected to exert its influence on the current order. The challenge for states such as Australia is to identify when Beijing's behaviour exceeds influence and begins to erode the system's liberal foundations.

China is already skilfully manoeuvring within international institutions to guide their operations, press for reforms and promote the China model. Four of the fifteen United Nations specialised agencies are run by Chinese nationals, including the Food and Agricultural Organization and the International Civil Aviation Organization. Ironically, the democratic nature of international institutions benefits Beijing. Chinese representatives in a variety of forums, such as the World Health Assembly and committees of the UN General Assembly, muster coalitions of the Global South to ensure favourable votes on issues such as Taiwan's (non)participation or to counter criticism of its repressive policies in Xinjiang.

China also elevates its government-organised NGOs, presenting an image of independence while drowning out the voices of independent civil society. The China Society for Human Rights Studies, for example, has official consultative status at the United Nations as an NGO, but is co-located with Chinese government offices and staffed by Chinese government officials, and has vigorously prosecuted China's human rights agenda.

The use of deft diplomacy and inducements to generate voting blocs is unsurprising. But China also seeks to change the system, diluting the liberal elements that threaten the China model and thus the CCP's rule.

For instance, China has already succeeded in weakening the liberal character of international human rights. In 2017, it proposed its first-ever resolution to the UN Human Rights Council, headed "The contribution of development to the enjoyment of all human rights".

It prioritised economic development above civil and political rights, and put the primacy of the state above the rights of the individual. Despite objections and nay votes from Western members, the resolution passed, and the subsequent report by the council's advisory committee, a body of eighteen experts supposed to maintain independence, referred mainly to Chinese Party-state documents.

The benefits of engaging with China's large economy will naturally draw countries into its political orbit

Chinese diplomats also block human rights resolutions at the UN Security Council, such as a February 2020 resolution on the plight of Myanmar's ethnic Rohingya. While the United States has arguably been similarly obstructive on resolutions about Palestine, it is for the narrow purpose of protecting an ally, rather than the broader project of weakening the rights themselves.

China has even been able to marshal the international system to defend and commend its behaviour in Xinjiang and Hong Kong. In 2019, at the 44th session of the UN Human Rights Council, a joint statement signed by twenty-seven countries, including Australia, expressed concern at arbitrary detention, widespread surveillance and restrictions in Xinjiang and the national security legislation in Hong Kong. A competing statement supporting the Hong Kong legislation received support from fifty-three states, only three of which are considered "free" by the non-governmental organisation Freedom House. By working within the system to rally a voting bloc, Beijing was able to compromise the world's peak human rights body. Tactics that have been successful in watering down human rights are now being employed in areas where norms are still being established, such as internet governance.

Inducements and intimidation

Much of China's effort to reshape the order comes through its ties with individual countries. Beijing uses its wealth and power to induce and coerce support for its positions, regardless of the corrosive impact on existing rules and norms.

A key source of inducements is the Belt and Road Initiative (BRI), Xi's signature foreign policy program. Aligning closely with the "right to development" China emphasised in its 2017 UN Human Rights Council resolution, the BRI deploys China's wealth and expertise to build a cross-national network of physical and digital connections with Beijing at its centre. Chinese loans finance construction, largely by Chinese companies, of the types of projects that have powered China's own economic success. A closer inspection of the countries supporting Hong Kong's national security legislation at the Human Rights Council finds that at least forty-three have signed on to the BRI.

China has also secured the United Nations' imprimatur for the BRI. In 2019, UN secretary-general António Guterres praised the BRI for its alignment with the UN's Sustainable Development Goals, earlier enshrined in a deal between the United Nations' development arm and Beijing.

Funding large infrastructure projects meets a legitimate demand in the developing world. It also offers political benefits for the partner governments, as Chinese loans can often help recipients defer painful economic reforms. But the risk is the accumulation of heavy debt burdens. A 2018 study by the think tank Center for Global Development identified at least eight countries where BRI projects had created issues of debt sustainability, including Laos, Pakistan and Mongolia.

The benefits of engaging with China's large economy will naturally draw countries into its political orbit. The BRI can also promote ideological security for Beijing, allowing it to tout the success of the China model, promote the right to development and suppress criticism. In contrast to what are seen as burdensome Western standards, China operates quickly and at the recipient country's discretion. As one senior Pacific bureaucrat put it: "We like China because they bring the red flags, not the red tape." Some BRI projects have been discredited for creating waste, corruption and crippling debt. But Chinese money – and the promise of an infrastructure-fuelled economic surge – will remain appealing.

A further risk is that China's economic engagement exacerbates illiberal pressures within other states and even bolsters dictators. Xi has said the China model offers "a new option for other countries and nations who want to speed up their development while preserving their independence". It could encourage countries to adopt a state-dominated economy or a repressive security apparatus. As Beijing looks to export internet infrastructure – a "digital silk road" – foreign leaders may be tempted to import toolkits for monitoring and censorship to manage security and political instability. Malaysia, for instance, is already using Chinese facial recognition software in its armed services, and Ethiopian government security services use Chinese equipment to surveil opposition activists and journalists.

Intimidation and coercion are the flipside of inducement, demonstrating the costs of displeasing China. There are numerous examples of this behaviour, such as "wolf warrior diplomacy", where PRC diplomats and officials defend Beijing's policies in aggressive and confrontational ways. In November 2019, China's ambassador to Sweden, Gui Congyou, said in a radio interview, "We treat our friends with fine wine, but for our enemies we have shotguns."

Australia was a primary target of Chinese ire after it led a call for an independent investigation into the origins of the COVID-19 pandemic. Together with launching a torrent of criticism from Chinese state media and officials, Beijing placed tariffs or bans on multiple Australian export sectors. Such coercion may only have hardened Australia's resolve, but, like wolf warrior diplomacy, it signals to the world that Beijing will not tolerate perceived threats to its ideological security.

China's truculence can also encourage a pre-emptive deference to its perceived interests. Beijing has used a mix of carrots and sticks to discourage South China Sea claimant states from asserting their rights, after ignoring a 2016 UN ruling rejecting its claims. Muting international criticism and disregarding the rule of law mirrors the tactics the CCP wields at home and undermines the foundations of the broader system.

Australia must acknowledge that the old order is gone … US power is fading

Beijing's effort to exert influence over other countries is especially effective where combined with its "united front work". These activities aim to promote a positive image of China and to stifle criticism by infiltrating domestic politics, the media and universities.

For Beijing, ideological challenges from "hostile forces at home and abroad" pose a threat, regardless of whether the forces are government actors. Its carrots and sticks serve to chill discourse among Chinese diasporas, dissidents and even businesses that value economic links with China. As professor of East Asian studies Perry Link wrote in 2002:

The Chinese government's censorial authority in recent times has resembled not so much a man-eating tiger or fire-snorting dragon as a giant anaconda coiled in an overhead chandelier. Normally the great snake doesn't move. It doesn't have to. It feels no need to be clear about its prohibitions. Its constant silent message is "You yourself decide," after which, more often than not, everyone in its shadow makes his or her large and small adjustments – all quite "naturally" … For years the intimidation was aimed only at Chinese citizens, but now it has been projected overseas.

This remains true nineteen years later. China aims to replicate its domestic playbook internationally and create an environment where not only governments, but also companies, groups and individuals defer to the Party's interests without being instructed to do so.

Resistance is not futile

Historically, Australia has been relatively successful at adapting to changes in the international order. But the confronting vision of 2049 sketched at the outset provides an unfamiliar challenge.

Australia must acknowledge that the old order is gone, to the extent that it was anchored in undisputed American primacy. US power is fading, and the globalisation it promotes has engendered the economic and cultural anxieties that have fuelled populist backlashes across the world. China's rise coincides with a moment of historic weakness of the current system.

The task for liberal democracies such as Australia is to balance two competing imperatives. One, the maintenance of an order with universal participation that enables cooperation on global challenges like climate change. Two, the preservation of universal values, reflecting liberal beliefs about the rule of law and individual rights.

Going too far in either direction is fraught. Prioritising participation could entrench illiberal norms as successive nations embrace elements of the China model. Prioritising values could bifurcate the international system and preclude global cooperation on existential challenges.

The space between is where a strategy emerges.

Liberal states must offer a positive vision to the region and the world, combined with a pointed critique of the Chinese alternative. Australia – through political leaders at home and diplomats abroad – must explicitly make the case that democratic institutions contribute more to national welfare and international peace and prosperity than any alternative. This is not an easy task. Like the China model, any liberal alternative is weakened by its own contradictions and hypocrisies, whether on the scale of the 2003 Iraq invasion, or overlooking undemocratic or illiberal politics in countries such as Vietnam and India in the name of security cooperation today. The public, too, must help to safeguard Australia's political system. Tolerating illiberalism at home only aids the authoritarian project to extinguish liberalism internationally.

Critiquing the China model can begin with exploiting the inherent contradictions in its pursuit of both ideological security and prosperity. Wolf warrior diplomacy and economic coercion may stifle some criticism, but these also create an image of Beijing as a bully and a threat, and undermine trade relationships and business confidence. Large China-funded infrastructure projects might burnish the credentials of the China model, but if they encourage corruption, damage the environment or fail to deliver promised benefits, Beijing risks being tarred as a careless or even exploitative imperial power.

This has already proven true: the more aggressive Beijing has been towards Taiwan, the more other countries have spoken up in its defence. While Beijing successfully excluded Taiwan from the 2020 World Health Assembly that met early in the COVID-19 crisis, an unprecedented number of countries were willing to advocate for Taiwan's inclusion.

Pushing back against the China model must begin with fostering resilience against the inducements and coercions of Chinese statecraft. Australia already offers a positive example of withstanding Chinese pressure since relations began to deteriorate in 2017. The debate in Australia about how to strengthen political institutions against foreign coercion and interference has been heated. At times, mistakes have been made. But to date Australia has largely preserved its values and independence. It has earned credibility for being unwilling to concede to Beijing's demands, and is well positioned to engage with other countries about building their own political resilience.

Often those nations with the strongest incentives to embrace China's economic engagement are the least equipped to manage risks to sovereignty or security. Australia, which has a strong and well-developed democracy, can provide solidarity and practical assistance when other countries face coercion from Beijing. It can also offer technical expertise on negotiating economic agreements with China. Most importantly, Australia can play a role in demonstrating the benefits of its political model, and in exposing the shortcomings of China's. The varied global responses to COVID-19, notably those of Australia, New Zealand and Taiwan, demonstrate that an authoritarian system is not the only model that can contain a pandemic.

Australia must choose its battles wisely – not every transgression can be resisted

Stronger democratic institutions in the region would ensure that, where engagement with China does not deliver, local political forces provide a corrective. Backlashes against governments perceived as being too close to China, and providing too little for their people, have occurred in Sri Lanka, Malaysia, Solomon Islands and Maldives. Robust domestic accountability could also encourage China to use methods less corrosive to liberalism, rather than prioritising coercion or bribery.

Even as China's increasing strength strains the liberal order, Australia can try to influence its behaviour. Promoting an agenda that aligns with China's is one method; pushing back and imposing costs is another. China's announcement that it will reach carbon neutrality before 2060, with greenhouse gas emissions peaking in the next decade, shows that alignment is possible. Although scant detail is available, this goal serves the domestic imperatives of China's leadership to reduce pollution and position the country for a green energy boom. But China played spoiler at the 2009 Copenhagen summit, and only signed on to the Paris Agreement after independent monitoring and reporting mechanisms were weakened. Its continued refusal to accept external accountability controls demonstrates the limits of an alignment strategy.

Markets and economic interests can also act as constraints. When China targeted South Korean businesses in 2017 in a dispute over a missile defence system, some lost billions. However, trade in industries most important to China's (and South Korea's) economic vitality was untouched, and overall South Korean exports actually increased that year. China's need to improve the quality of life for its population will often be weighed against its strategic considerations. China's deep level of interdependence with the rest of the world remains a major opportunity for aligning incentives.

A disciplined Biden administration could serve to rally allies and partners in a way that the incoherent and unreliable Trump administration could not. Countries such as Australia have little to no ability to impose costs on China unilaterally. While there may be safety in numbers, imposing costs risks an escalation in Chinese aggression. Australia must therefore choose its battles wisely – not every transgression can be resisted. It should begin by working with partner states to develop clear parameters of unacceptable behaviour, particularly on industrial and cyber espionage, foreign interference and egregious human rights violations. New opportunities for such coalitions are emerging through the growth of minilateral diplomacy, including the expanding scope of Five Eyes discussions, the Quad and the ASEAN–Australia Special Summit. Just as importantly, agreed stances could incorporate each partner's tolerance for risk and countenance a diverse array of tools: diplomacy, carrots and sticks will all have a role to play.

Preparing for the new world disorder

The history of liberal internationalism is replete with contradictions. Some say that in recent decades it is Washington, not Beijing, which has damaged the order most. So can China really do more damage to an order already on life support? Liberalism is not just facing an external challenge, but one from within.

The answer requires optimism about liberalism's capacity to self-correct across the arc of history, and scepticism that illiberalism can do likewise. In 2020, America's struggles with healthcare, gun policy and race relations were exposed like never before, but the openness that revealed these systemic failures itself represents an underlying strength. As much as Donald Trump belittled, criticised and attacked America's institutions, he also created the conditions for a course correction – Joe Biden's victory.

Even in Trump's America, journalists uncovered tax records and found evidence for two impeachments, activists rallied and a coalition mobilised to vote Trump from office. The American story, echoed across liberal democracies, is one of grievance-fuelled self-harm, but also of accountability, political contestation and – for the optimistic among us – renewal.

Contrast this with China. Journalists attempting the same kind of investigative reporting on the CCP would find themselves imprisoned or expelled. Whereas the world mocked Trump's media appearances during the COVID-19 pandemic (remember injecting bleach?), not once did Xi Jinping appear before the press to defend or promote his actions. In fact, citizen journalists who reported on the early days of the crisis in Wuhan disappeared.

The CCP is a well-resourced and well-organised political force. It has the potential to be far more effective than any iconoclastic but capricious populist in permanently weakening the liberal foundations of the global order. Much of China's influence abroad is unavoidable. A rising power with the economic and military strength that China wields is unlikely to be deterred.

On this logic, optimism has no place. Disorder is the most likely trajectory for the international system – a world that is more chaotic and less institutionalised.

But it would also be mistaken to adopt a fatalistic approach. Instead, Australia and its partners must focus their efforts on those elements of the liberal order most worth preserving and most under threat. Australia can and must prepare for a world where an alternative value system rises to challenge liberalism head on. The centenary of the People's Republic is still twenty-eight years away. ■

The authors would like to thank Nadège Rolland, Richard McGregor, Allan Gyngell, Richard Maude, Nathan Attrill and Victor Ferguson for their useful comments.

THE TRUCE

Negotiating the end of the American era

Sam Roggeveen

It is difficult to say exactly when the Cold War began, but 12 March 1947 is a fitting enough marker. This was the date on which President Harry Truman told a joint session of Congress and a national radio audience that "[i]t must be the policy of the United States to support free peoples who are resisting attempted subjugation by armed minorities or by outside pressures". The announcement of the Truman Doctrine, as it came to be known, inaugurated America's worldwide struggle against communism. It was soon followed by the Marshall Plan to rebuild Western Europe, the founding of NATO, the creation of the Defense Department (and, with it, a dramatic reversal of postwar military demobilisation) and the start of the Korean War. And that only takes us to 1950.

In comparison, what can we say about the new Cold War, the one America and China are now alleged to be fighting? When did the United States launch a global struggle for influence with the emerging Asian superpower? We might choose 17 November 2011, when President Barack Obama announced America's pivot to Asia in a speech to the Australian parliament. But the pivot was never properly resourced, and it is former president Donald Trump who has been credited with systematically shifting the focus of the US security apparatus to great-power competition. So a more fitting date to mark Washington's inauguration of this competition would be 18 December 2017, the day the Trump administration released its National Security Strategy and labelled China a "strategic competitor" that "seeks to displace the United States in the Indo-Pacific region".

This means that if Cold War II is underway, we are a little over three years into it. In these three years, we have seen the United States announce it is entering an era of competition with China, introduce anti-China tariffs and criticise China in firebrand speeches by then vice-president Mike Pence ("China wants nothing less than to push the United States of America from the Western Pacific and attempt to prevent us from coming to the aid of our allies. But they will fail") and then secretary of state Mike Pompeo ("The free world must triumph over this new tyranny"). The United States has also pushed back against Chinese foreign interference and launched a largely successful campaign to convince friends and allies about the risks of dealing with Chinese telecommunications giant Huawei.

This does not amount to anything comparable to what Truman set in motion in the first three years of the original Cold War. Of course, history never repeats exactly, but if this really is a new Cold

War, we might by now expect to have heard a major national address from the US president declaring China the enemy of all free people and inaugurating a new doctrine to combat its malign influence. We might have seen a large increase in defence spending and a dramatic migration of US military forces to the Pacific, and perhaps a signature diplomatic initiative and an accompanying trade pact to bring together Asian nations that feel threatened by Beijing. And instead of the suspension of the trade war in January 2020, when the United States and China signed the first of what both sides promised would be several new trade deals, we might have seen an escalation.

None of this has happened. If America is fighting a Cold War against China, it is off to a slow start.

The China challenge

The absence of an American show of military and diplomatic strength is not for want of Chinese provocation. The charge sheet of China's offences against international rules and norms is by now familiar: illegal expansion of its territory and maritime zone in the South China Sea, industrial-scale theft of foreign intellectual property, intimidation of trading partners with threats of economic blackmail, massive expansion of military capacity and reach, cyberattacks against foreign countries (including Australia) and trampling on Hong Kong's freedoms through the introduction of a new security law. Then there is the Belt and Road Initiative, which some Western experts fear is not so much an infrastructure project as a grand design to tie clients to a

Beijing-centred political and economic order. We should also assume that China aims to displace the United States as the leading power in Asia, and ultimately seeks to pressure the United States to dissolve its alliances and remove its military forces from the region. No great power wants its region to be dominated by a rival.

So much for China's actions and ambitions. What really ought to have provoked a major response from the United States by now is China's *potential*. Again, the contrast with the Cold War is stark. The Soviet Union, let us recall, was a broken nation in the early Cold War years, economically prostrate and physically devastated by Stalin's collectivisation (12 million or perhaps as many as 20 million dead) and Hitler's

Trump made no decisive difference to the direction of events . . . Biden won't either

aggression (26 million dead). Yet so seriously did the Truman administration take the threat from the USSR in 1947 that it inaugurated a doctrine of permanent global confrontation and initiated a massive rearmament program. China, by contrast, hasn't been to war in more than forty years, and its last catastrophic internal purge, the Cultural Revolution, is now forty-five years behind it. China has enjoyed four decades of rapid economic growth and is on its way to becoming the richest nation on the planet. In the last twenty years, it has embarked on a military modernisation effort with few contemporary parallels while spending only about 2 per cent of its GDP on the military.

How is it, then, that the United States has been so slow to confront China with the same resolve it showed against the Soviets under Truman? True, Trump was no Truman, but this misses the point. Trump's leadership made no decisive difference to the direction of events because the scale and nature of those events would have made it difficult for any president to emulate Truman. For the same reason, Joe Biden won't make a decisive difference either.

Why America won't fight China

To put America's dilemma in a few words, the problem is that the job is too big and the stakes too small. The job is too big because military power is a function of economic power, and China's economy is enormous. In 1991 it was roughly the same size as Australia's, yet by 2019 it was roughly two-thirds the size of the US economy. According to World Bank figures released in May 2020, in purchasing power parity terms, China's economic output now accounts for 16.4 per cent of global output, while the United States contributes 16.3 per cent. That means Beijing can challenge American military primacy in Asia without bankrupting itself, unlike the Soviet Union. What's more, China can focus all that military power on its region because, unlike the United States, it chooses not to spread its military resources across the globe.

Since the end of the Cold War, American military power in the Asia-Pacific has been built on its navy, which had the ability to roam the region and operate across vast distances with little fear of interference.

In 1996, the Clinton administration's sailing of a carrier battlegroup and an amphibious assault fleet through the Taiwan Strait to demonstrate its support for Taiwan and its opposition to Chinese military intimidation against Taipei was the material expression of this supremacy. US military leaders were clearly confident that, in the event relations with Beijing deteriorated into a military clash, the US Navy could not only defend itself against anything China could throw at it, but also use its fleet to project significant military power to the Chinese mainland.

The United States can feel no such assurance today. China now has the world's largest navy, according to the Pentagon's annual assessment of the People's Liberation Army, and its capability is second only to that of the United States. It has developed an array of new missiles – and the ships, submarines and aircraft to carry them – which make it impossible for the US Navy to operate close to China's shores at reasonable risk. In a conflict between China and Taiwan, US intervention would now be unacceptably costly. The United States would risk losing not only its aircraft carriers but also its bases in Japan and Guam. And what is true for Taiwan is becoming true of Asia more broadly – as China's maritime power grows and is projected further outward, the shift from US military supremacy to a military balance expands throughout the region.

Yet even though China is the most serious threat to America's leadership in Asia since World War II, that is still not a good enough reason for America to fight for it. Firstly, the ideological justification is missing – the Chinese Communist Party (CCP) clearly takes its ideology very seriously, but it is not at the vanguard of a global movement to overthrow democratic capitalism, as the Soviet Union once was. China is beginning to promote its development model to the world, but it doesn't offer a set of universal values that compete with liberal ideas. The economic justification is weak too – even if China forced the United States to withdraw all its military forces from Asia, this wouldn't cut America out of Asia economically because the costs of doing so would be prohibitive. The Lowy Institute's Asia Power Index shows that in the decade to 2019 alone, new American investment in Asia totalled US$511 billion, versus US$413 billion for next-placed Japan. That level of economic integration cannot be easily undone, and it would be disastrous to try.

Lastly, there is no existential justification for America to oppose China's rise because neither the United States nor China poses a direct threat to the other's landmass. They are far enough apart, and each has a large enough army and nuclear arsenal, to make them safe from invasion. Of course, the United States defines its interests more broadly than that. As strategist Bruno Maçães puts it, "Since it became a world power around 1900, the United States had one permanent strategic goal: to prevent a single power from controlling the whole of Eurasia." But despite China's size, it has no prospect of dominating the Eurasian landmass because it is surrounded by great powers, of which the United States is just one.

Nevertheless, America's mood regarding China has shifted. *Financial Times* columnist Martin Wolf wrote in 2019 that "[a]cross-the-board rivalry with China is becoming an organising principle of US economic, foreign and security policies". What's remarkable about this shift is how little consideration has apparently been given to whether it is a good idea. The consensus that the United States and China are in competition for the leadership of Asia has developed so rapidly that the question of whether it is desirable has been sidelined. Yet confronting China in a whole-of-government contest for leadership in Asia would be so costly, and the prize so elusive and insubstantial, that it is a choice no rational American leader could make.

Right now, the United States is in the worst of all worlds. It has committed itself rhetorically to a Cold War–style struggle against China, but without the resolve to wage it and with no realistic sense of the sacrifices it will demand. So

> **The attempt to liberalise China by exposing it to Western goods and ideas has comprehensively failed**

although there is growing understanding in Washington about the significance of China's rise (a belated realisation deferred by almost two decades of fixation on Islamist terrorism), what's missing is a willingness to admit that a highly advantageous distribution of power that seemed permanent is in fact temporary, and that it is not in America's interest to prevent the shift away from US leadership in Asia.

The limits of liberalism

Underlying that reluctance is a sense that modern China, led by the CCP, is not entirely legitimate. A wealthy, authoritarian China is a standing rebuke to the post–Cold War Western consensus that the world was moving inexorably towards the embrace of liberal democracy, and that this was the only guaranteed pathway to international good citizenship and economic prosperity. But the United States misinterpreted the collapse of the Soviet Union as a global victory for Western liberalism when it really only marked the defeat of communism in Europe. Four of the five communist countries left on Earth are Asian (China, North Korea, Vietnam and Laos). As economist Adam Tooze recently wrote, the West didn't win the Cold War in Asia. The Korean War was fought to a stalemate that endures to this day, the Vietnam War was lost and, most importantly, China avoided the fate of European communism in the late 1980s and thereafter thrived. The liberal rules-based order that the United States champions is a largely transatlantic Cold War phenomenon too; America's Asian Cold War was marked by close cooperation with authoritarian governments in South Vietnam, South Korea, Taiwan, the Philippines and Indonesia. In sum, when it comes to the Cold War in Asia, the United States can really only claim a draw.

Yet liberal universalism has been a signature feature of post–Cold War American foreign policy and rhetoric. President Bill Clinton said of China's accession to the World Trade Organization in 2001, "The more China liberalizes its economy, the more fully it will liberate the potential of its people ... And when individuals have the power, not just to dream but to realize their dreams, they will demand a greater say." In his second inaugural address in 2004, President George W. Bush said, "The best hope for peace in our world is the expansion of freedom in all the world … So it is the policy of the United States to seek and support the growth of democratic movements and institutions in every nation and culture, with the ultimate goal of ending tyranny in our world." When President Barack Obama launched the pivot to Asia in Canberra in 2011, he said: "Every nation will chart its own course. Yet it is also true that certain rights are universal; among them, freedom of speech, freedom of the press, freedom of assembly, freedom of religion, and the freedom of citizens to choose their own leaders."

Whether President Biden pursues such an agenda will tell us much about how America now sees itself and its relations with Beijing, and whether its views on China's legitimacy are evolving. The Brookings Institution's Thomas Wright says that some of Biden's advisers want "the United States to make democratic cooperation an organizing principle of its foreign policy, partly as a means of competing with China and partly because they believe that democracy itself is at grave risk", but others worry about creating an ideological fault line that damages relations with Beijing. Before the election, Biden committed to hosting a Summit for Democracy in his first year "to put strengthening democracy back on the global stage". Perhaps this conference will set the path for an ideological confrontation with China, but the tone of the proposal suggests it is focused on defending democratic norms against interference from abroad and populist threats at home rather than on advancing them in China and elsewhere.

That defensiveness is consistent with a change of mood in Washington about China's political system. Since Xi Jinping assumed leadership in 2012, he has tightened control over public speech and reinforced the ideological leadership of the CCP. Xi's apparent success has led to growing pessimism in Washington that political change will occur in China. The failure of the Arab Spring in 2011 had already dealt a blow to the techno-optimists who thought Twitter and Facebook could be a force for political liberation; China's apparent success at suppressing online dissent reinforced the point. China under Xi looks increasingly like a state that has found the formula for combining capitalism with tight political control.

Rather than interpreting this as a signal to urgently redouble its democratisation effort or to simply give free trade and the information revolution more time to do their work, the conventional wisdom in Washington now is that the attempt to liberalise China by exposing it to Western goods and ideas has comprehensively failed. The 2017 National Security Strategy acknowledged the point: "For decades, U.S. policy was rooted in the belief that support for China's rise and for its integration into the postwar international order would liberalize China. Contrary to our hopes, China expanded its power at the expense of the sovereignty of others." In a March 2018 article in US journal *Foreign Affairs*, Kurt Campbell, former assistant secretary of state for East Asian and Pacific affairs, and Ely Ratner, vice-president Joe Biden's deputy national security adviser, concurred, arguing that the United States had "put too much faith in its power to shape China's trajectory". Campbell is now Biden's coordinator for the Indo-Pacific, and Ratner is the Pentagon's principal adviser on China.

This re-evaluation marks a significant acknowledgement – that economic prosperity *is* possible under an authoritarian government. The United States insisted throughout the Cold War that democracy and prosperity were inextricably linked; victory in the Cold War re-inforced this belief, and it was cemented by the post–Cold War fate of Eastern Europe, where new democracies that embraced the free market prospered, while authoritarian Russia and the former Soviet republics stagnated. Yet China's rise has led Washington to rethink its assumptions. Communist China is no longer seen as an aberration or a recalcitrant hold-out against democratic modernity, like a giant North Korea or Iran. It is, rather, a permanent and legitimate power centre in the international system that must be treated as an equal.

What China wants is an end to liberal universalism, not an end to liberalism

An ideological truce

This is a timely shift. As we have seen, America cannot win a contest with China for supremacy in Asia – it lacks the resolve, because China is insufficiently threatening to its core interests, and the spoils of victory too ephemeral. Moreover, America's supporters in Asia don't want such a contest. All are concerned about the implications of China's rise. Some nations have chosen to bandwagon with Beijing, while others develop countermeasures that will make it harder for China to coerce them. But China is a leading trading partner for all of them, and a growing part of their economic future – and none of them can have any realistic fear that China seeks to convert them to communism because China shows no inclination to export its ideology. So an ideological battle that pits liberal-democratic ideals against the CCP's will raise the stakes of the contest when it is very much in America's interest, and those of its allies and friends in Asia, to lower them.

There is good reason to think that China would be satisfied with an ideological truce. What China wants is an end to liberal universalism, not an end to liberalism – it doesn't want to convert democracies and it doesn't care much about liberal values, so long as they don't infect China. Strategist Nadège Rolland argues that "[i]nstead of the liberal uniformity sought by the United States – individual liberty, free expression, economic liberalism, and democracy – the Chinese elites envisage a world where authoritarian regimes and the prominent role of the state are not stigmatized". Similarly, writer Tanner Greer says China wants the United States and its Western friends and allies to give up on the idea that its values are universal:

Democratization, free markets, and universal human rights would no longer be enshrined as the bedrock of the world's most important international institutions or be seen as the default standards of good governance. They would instead be reduced to a parochial tradition peculiar to a smattering of outcast Western nations.

Stripped of pejorative language, this sounds like a deal the United States and its friends and allies should be able to live with. After all, this "smattering of outcast Western nations" – Europe and the United Kingdom, North America, Japan, South Korea and Australia, among others – is actually a huge portion of the world's economy and has massive diplomatic and military clout.

Moreover, to describe democracy, free markets and human rights as the "bedrock" of international institutions is an overstatement. The United Nations, for instance, is in certain guises an idealistic institution that encourages the international community to move towards the liberal-democratic ideals embodied in the Declaration of Human Rights. But those ambitions fall largely to the wayside in the Security Council, a forum for great-power politics that would not have looked unfamiliar to the statesmen who attended the Congress of Vienna in 1814–15. As for free trade, China has a mixed record. The Heritage Foundation's Index of Economic Freedom shows that China has made enormous progress on trade since the mid-1990s and is now considered "mostly free". The index also measures investment freedom (the domestic and international constraints on the flow of investment capital), and here China's score went from 50 ("repressed") in 1995 to 20 in 2019. But the international architecture of free trade – the international bodies, regional trade deals and bilateral preferential agreements – has long been rickety, shot through with contradictions and national exceptions. China's inconsistency is hardly exceptional, and at the very least we can say that China is not a committed ideological opponent of economic globalisation. Then there are the multilateral institutions that are critical to maintaining international peace and commerce – everything from the International Atomic Energy Agency to the International Telecommunication Union and the Bank for International Settlements. Each serves as a stage for power politics, but none has a clear ideological motivation. In other words, the institutions that form the core of diplomatic relations between states won't suddenly be compromised if the United States and the West stop investing them with missionary liberal purpose.

All in all, the United States and China would both benefit by backing away from ideological conflict. That could be achieved informally, but Greer makes the novel proposal to formalise it through an "ideological disarmament agreement" in which both sides would agree to dismantle bodies such as the National Endowment for Democracy in the United States and the United Front Work Department in China, and end rhetorical support for ideological causes abroad. For the United States, it would be a dramatic step to openly abandon the missionary purpose with which it has been invested since its founding. But the Trump presidency should remind us of the possibility of radical change to America's perception of its role in the world, and such a shift is exactly what the present moment calls for. An ideological disarmament agreement won't secure peace between the two great powers by itself, but it would mark a mutual acknowledgement that each side sees the other's political system as legitimate and untouchable, and thus could serve as the foundation for a long truce.

Biden's mission

Even without such an agreement, the temper of the foreign policy debate in the United States suggests that America won't press an ideological agenda because it has lost confidence in its ability to spread liberalism and has acknowledged the legitimacy and longevity of the Chinese model. Yet Joe Biden belongs to a generation of political leaders who put liberal values at the centre of their conception of America's place in the world, so

Peace is more likely if Washington thinks of itself as an ordinary great power

it remains an open question whether he has internalised Washington's new pessimism. Biden might also be out of sync with the establishment in one other significant respect: China's strength. After many years of distraction in the Middle East, Washington now seems to understand the full implications of China's economic growth and the strategic power that goes with it. But in an October 2020 interview, Biden nominated Russia as America's biggest security threat, with China merely a "competitor". In May 2019, Biden had been even more dismissive, saying, "They're not competition for us," claiming that China is too corrupt and has too few natural resources to compete with the United States.

Ideological overconfidence, combined with a poor grasp of China's true size and capability, could make for a dangerous four years. Whether nations choose to go to war will always be a leader's judgement, and one of the decisive questions they ask themselves before committing military forces is: "Can we win?" Should the United States and China find themselves in a confrontation over Taiwan or in the South China Sea, this question will arise. We should all hope that when this moment comes, the US president appreciates his adversary's strengths.

Many criticisms can be made of Donald Trump's foreign policy, but he did at least regard China as a peer. Trump was also candid about his own nation's shortcomings. In a 2017 interview, when he was confronted with Russian president Vladimir Putin's brutality, including the assassination of political opponents, Trump responded: "You think our country's so innocent?" It is impossible to imagine Biden uttering those words; impossible even to imagine the thought entering his mind. Yet when it comes to the future of US–China relations, Trump's sentiment fits the moment better: war is less likely if both sides have a realistic understanding of each other's strengths, and peace is more likely if Washington thinks of itself as an ordinary great power, rather than anointed with a mission to bring freedom and democracy to the world. ■

MIDDLE-POWER MIGHT

A plan for dealing with China

Linda Jaivin

Mao once said: "All under heaven is in chaos; the situation is excellent."
By those standards, 2020 was a thoroughly excellent year. Australia and California burned, Arctic sea ice cover shrank and the sixth mass extinction continued apace as the climate crisis accelerated. The COVID-19 pandemic sparked what *The Economist* called the "deepest, most synchronised collapse" of the global economy on record. All this took place against a rise in autocracy and an ongoing crisis in liberal democracy, most spectacularly in the United States.

To add to Australia's woes, as 2020 wound up, its relationship with the People's Republic of China (PRC) appeared to be slipping onto life support. This was the case even before Zhao Lijian, a Chinese foreign ministry vice-spokesperson, tweeted a doctored photo purporting to show a smiling Australian soldier slitting an Afghan child's throat. Prime Minister Scott Morrison demanded an apology.

"Apologise to the Afghan people" came the answer. The Australian government had already done so. Zhao almost certainly knew that, but was grandstanding for his home audience. That Australia-bashing has become a way for Party hacks and performative patriots to score political points in China is a dispiriting development.

Earlier in the year, the Morrison government's unilateral call for an inquiry into the origins of the pandemic, with World Health Organization investigators to be given "weapons inspector"–style powers, and Peter Dutton's dark mutterings about (non-existent) US "documentation" on the pandemic's suspicious origins pushed the relationship, already strained, closer towards a cliff's edge. Deriding Canberra as a "loyal attack dog" for the United States – a "paper cat" to America's "paper tiger" – the reliably snarky *Global Times* warned that "Australia has $153.2 billion reasons not to pick a fight with China". Soon came the proof. Beijing advised its students to think twice about going to "racist" and "dangerous" Australia for their education. By year's end, Beijing had slapped heavy tariffs on Australian barley and wine, limited beef imports and extended the punishments to coal, cotton, copper, sugar and lobsters. When Australian ministers called to discuss, their Chinese counterparts refused to pick up the phone.

In each case, the CCP's retributive actions came with plausible deniability: the Chinese side referred to established processes or ongoing investigations (about the alleged dumping of wine, for example, or problems with the labelling of the beef) or domestic policies, such as achieving self-sufficiency in coal production. Should the CCP decide to reverse course, it can do so without loss of face.

Last year also saw Chinese security agents arbitrarily detain the television presenter Cheng Lei, an Australian who worked for Chinese state media, and charge another Australian, imprisoned writer Yang Hengjun, with espionage. The last two journalists representing the Australian media in China, the ABC's Bill Birtles and the *Australian Financial Review*'s Mike Smith, felt threatened enough to flee.

Central to the story of the deterioration in Australia–China relations has been the rise of Xi Jinping. China's supreme leader is also its most autocratic since Mao, and exceptionally sensitive to criticism – as the considerable number of his imprisoned critics in China can attest. Xi's harshest

Wherever there's a rules-based order, [China] now wants to write the rules

critics within (or recently evicted from) the Party may be right when they say that 70 per cent of China's 92 million Party members oppose his leadership. They may be wrong; it's impossible to say. As for the other 1.4 billion Chinese citizens: who knows? The PRC doesn't do independent polling. The fact that it spends more on maintaining domestic "stability" through policing and surveillance than on defence says something about the balance of coercion and co-optation.

The Xi era, China historian Geremie Barmé has written, combines "the vitriol, hysteria and violent intent" of the Mao era with "the forensic detail afforded by digital surveillance". Xi has ruthlessly dispatched factional enemies and rivals under the credible cover of his anti-corruption campaign, crushed China's nascent civil society and stomped out dissent, while expanding both censorship and demands for ideological conformity. He doesn't care what the world thinks about what he is doing in Xinjiang and Tibet, or on the issue of Taiwan; he does, however, care what it says.

Xi is able to do what he wants because the PRC today is not just a global economic, manufacturing and technological powerhouse, a key player in multilateral institutions and a provider of infrastructure and aid to the developing world, but a "combat-ready" military power eager to demonstrate its prowess. Whether in the context of the UN Council of Human Rights, the South China Sea or the Taiwan Strait, wherever there's a rules-based order, it now wants to write the rules – to make the world, in the words of Yale professor Jessica Chen Weiss, "safe for autocracy".

This poses unique challenges for Australia, with its geographical proximity to and economic dependency on the PRC. We need to sharpen our game. This will depend partly on improving the way we deal with the outside world, including taking advantage of opportunities for multilateral cooperation and solidarity in the face of attempted coercion. It will depend, too, on boosting our diplomatic resources and raising the level of "China literacy" within the Australian community, public service and government. And it will rely, to an extent that has not yet been widely recognised, on strengthening our own democratic practices and institutions.

The shrimp's dilemma

During his tenure, Donald Trump turned the United States into an unstable and dangerous ally. American rhetoric towards China took an especially dangerous turn when Secretary of State Mike Pompeo all but called for regime change in the PRC. (It went so well in Korea, Vietnam, Chile, Afghanistan and Iraq, after all.) In July 2020, Pompeo declared that the United States must "engage and empower the Chinese people – a dynamic, freedom-loving people who are completely distinct from the Chinese Communist Party". He added: "But changing the CCP's behaviour cannot be the mission of the Chinese people alone. Free nations have to work to defend freedom." Australia's greatest security partner was, in effect, pledging to commit reckless adventurism against our biggest trading partner. As a Korean proverb has it, when two whales quarrel, it's the shrimp's back that gets broken.

The election of Joe Biden, who has spoken of building "a united front of US allies and partners to confront China's abusive behaviours and human rights violations", is no guarantee that existing tensions between China and the United States will be easily or quickly resolved. He may well bring some stability to US foreign policy, and he advocates cooperation with Beijing on issues where interests "converge". But there remain many points of friction. There will be ongoing pressure on Canberra to stand with the United States should rhetorical push come to military shove – if it does, it will only confirm Beijing's contemptuous belief that Canberra takes its marching orders from Washington.

Taiwan is a likely flashpoint. In early 2020, on commencing her second term as president after a landslide victory at the polls, Tsai Ing-wen remarked that there was no need for Taiwan to declare independence because "we are an independent country already". Taiwan independence is a major red line for Beijing, which immediately ramped up its military posturing in the Taiwan Strait. Should the PRC decide to attack or invade Taiwan, and the United States steps in, this little Australian shrimp had better have a plan.

Brendan Taylor, professor of strategic studies at the Australian National University, says that in any conflict over Taiwan, "The Americans would primarily be interested in our involvement for its symbolic value." They might want Australian submarines to help enforce a "distant blockade" to control the "choke points" through which Chinese ships convey vital imports of oil. The United States could also be interested in our EA-18G Growler electronic warfare fighter jets – we have eleven, the only country outside America with them. Taylor recommends the urgent establishment of multilateral "risk avoidance and crisis management mechanisms", such as those now in place on the Korean Peninsula, as well as a dedicated task force in Canberra with personnel drawn from the Department of Foreign Affairs and Trade and the Department of Defence.

I would add defence historians and China specialists to the task force as well. This would help us to learn the lessons from incidents such as that in 1996, when Australia supported the dispatch of US naval forces into the Taiwan Strait in response to Chinese missile tests, and to better comprehend the CCP's red lines and rhetoric. When it comes to China, history is always relevant. Or as the educator Yuen Ren Chao famously remarked to Bertrand Russell in 1920 when the English philosopher, who was visiting China, told him he was working on an essay titled "Causes of the Present Chaos", "The cause of the present chaos is past chaos."

A bipartisan, expertly staffed task force wouldn't be a bad idea for advising on the Australia–China relationship more broadly.

Middle-power superpowers

Australia is in a difficult position with China. Beijing's goodwill is in short supply, with its spokespeople issuing strong warnings about what they describe as Canberra's "confrontational" new defence pact with Tokyo. Towards the end of 2020, Beijing's ambassador to Australia revealed "fourteen disputes" between Australia and the PRC, ranging from accusations that China is conducting cyberattacks on Australian targets to the Morrison government's attempts to "torpedo" Victoria's Belt and Road deal to "unfriendly or antagonistic" commentary on China in parliament and independent media. According to Beijing's foreign ministry, "whoever hung the bell on the tiger's neck must untie it" – whoever began the trouble should end it. In their view, this is Australia.

In August 2020, Morrison pledged his government to "strategic patience and consistency" in its "mutually beneficial" relationship with China, while safeguarding national sovereignty and security. Yet he himself has not always shown "strategic patience" or "consistency".

A former high-ranking diplomat points out that Morrison's quick-draw response to Zhao Lijian's offensive tweet only served to dignify it (Zhao is a relatively minor, if noisy, official) and back Australia into a corner. Similarly, a cleverer response to the list of China's fourteen complaints about Australia would have been, says the diplomat, to say, *Great, this clears the air. Let's talk. We'd like to understand your position better and have you understand ours.* Australia could adhere to its principles while defusing the tension. And if China doesn't want to talk, that's on them.

Australia could do worse than to study the kind of principled pragmatism that guides Asian countries such as Singapore in their relations with China. Singaporean prime minister Lee Hsien Loong has observed that the PRC's foreign policies, like those of the United States, may be both impelled and constrained by "powerful domestic pressures", rather than "rational calculations" of national interest. Singapore aims for good relations with both the United States and the PRC – but is ever mindful of the "reality on the doorstep" that is China.

For Australia, dealing with that "reality on the doorstep" means acknowledging the limitations and advantages of being a middle power so as not to become just a stuck-in-the-middle power. This involves recognising that China literacy and engagement (which former US ambassador to China Winston Lord calls "a tactic, not a strategy") are middle-power superpowers. As former diplomat and DFAT secretary Peter Varghese suggests, even if a comprehensive strategic partnership is not possible with a "one-party authoritarian state", it is unwise to "treat the PRC as an enemy". Rather than try to contain China, Australia ought to "engage and constrain".

China literacy means understanding that many Chinese people may be "freedom-loving", as Pompeo claimed, but that doesn't automatically equate to "America-loving". Even among those who do love America, cherish some ideal of democracy, or are simply mad for Hollywood or Apple computers, few would welcome US-led regime change. If China is to change, it must be the Chinese who change it.

As suggested above, not even every member of the CCP buys the Party line – otherwise, the CCP wouldn't need to issue regulations, as it did in 2020, banning members from deviating from this line even in private conver-

Australia could do worse than to study the kind of principled pragmatism that guides China

sations. It would, however, be folly not to take CCP pronouncements seriously or to underestimate the strength, breadth and sincerity of patriotic sentiment in China. The Party's most fervent supporters, the flag-waving "little pinks", macho "wolf warriors" and foot-stamping "patriotic fangirls", might present like the love children of *South Park* and North Korea. But not all Chinese nationalists are so cartoonish, and the CCP, which represents 6.6 per cent of the population, cannot be unpicked easily from the fabric of greater Chinese society. Party members hold important positions in every significant business and public institution, university and school.

Even Party members may be mildly democracy-curious, or, like members of the broader society, also interested in other things, such as sci-fi, rock music, viniculture, photographing themselves in ancient costume or livestreaming their farm work (a thing). Part of being China literate is to perceive China as a multitude, irreducible to the CCP, economic growth figures, military posturing or speeches by Xi Jinping. It's also true that many more people apply for CCP membership each year than are accepted, and of those admitted to the Party in 2019, four out of five were millennials.

China literacy requires strong institutional support for the study of Chinese history, politics, language and culture at the tertiary level – some of the very courses imperilled by the Australian government's recent short-sighted "reforms" to the university sector. Sinology is not Sinophilia, no matter how often the two are accidently (or maliciously) conflated. The old model of "China watching", conducted by China-interested but Chinese-illiterate observers who rely on select "informants", can never substitute for deep knowledge of China in all its complexity and historical depth. Graduates in China-related studies have made significant contributions in diplomacy, business, public health, disaster relief, cultural exchange, law and journalism, engaging with the PRC while growing the pool of Australian expertise on China. Such engagement means that in times of tension – as are inevitable, given the disparity in political systems and alliances – there are still open channels of communication.

Diplomacy is central to this project. Aid is also important, not just in terms of managing the relationship with China but also in consolidating our ties with countries throughout the Asia-Pacific. The Coalition's cuts to the budget for diplomacy and aid – down from a high of $5 billion under Gillard in 2012–2013 to $4 billion under Morrison in 2019–20 – are own goals. For cost-cutting measures, they carry a potentially high price tag, especially as China expands its influence in the region, assiduously filling the holes we've left.

Engagement does not mean ignoring the near-continuous threats to national security by what China expert Anne-Marie Brady calls the PRC's "party-state-military-market nexus", from cyberattacks to old-fashioned espionage.

China literacy and engagement are the middle power's superpowers

It does involve creating space for conversations to be conducted outside shouty cyberspace or other public spheres. While taking part in academic and cultural exchanges in the past, I've had frank, in-depth conversations with Chinese officials and CCP members who genuinely wanted to understand why, for example, the West is so concerned about the detention of dissidents, or how a country's citizens can feel united under a democratic system that pits political parties and their followers against one another in heated political debate. Conversations like this contribute, incrementally but cumulatively and significantly, to mutual understanding – as does having

Chinese students studying at Australian universities, and vice versa, as well as collaborations between Chinese and Australian researchers. The head of Universities Australia, Catriona Jackson, notes our dependence on such partnerships: "Without research collaboration – remember we're quite a small population – we are in really serious trouble."

It is true that the CCP wants everyone, from classrooms to the streets, to stop criticising its policies in Hong Kong, Tibet and Xinjiang; to follow its rules on how to speak about Taiwan; and to only publish maps that accord with its view of territoriality. It is demanding that the entire planet becomes its "safe space", which makes the CCP the world's biggest snowflake. Yet what happens on Australian soil is governed by Australian law. The CCP is not ignorant of this fact; it just doesn't like it.

Universities and other research institutions do need to exercise diligence to ensure that collaborations don't involve the transfer of sensitive technology. It is well documented that some Chinese students monitor, intimidate and report on peers who dare to express opinions that clash with the Party line. Universities must defend free speech and inquiry. There has to be zero tolerance for threatening behaviour, with expulsion a possibility. Incitement to violence should automatically be referred to the police.

The University of Oxford has instituted a system whereby essays in Chinese studies subjects are submitted anonymously, and has made it an offence to record classes or share them online. Tutorials, in some cases, take place one-on-one instead of in groups. It is unfortunate but, with Chinese embassies maintaining online portals for informants, necessary and sensible. Our universities could consider similar regimes.

The government can harden the spines of our university administrators by restoring the money it has stripped from their budgets. The problems on campuses will remain intractable so long as the tertiary sector is forced to rely on international students for survival. The fallout from COVID-19 border closures might prove a useful circuit breaker. The Morrison government's ongoing culture wars, however, signal that the self-sabotaging denial of support for universities in general and attack on the liberal arts in particular will continue.

If China literacy and engagement are the middle power's superpowers, a Cold Warrior mindset is its kryptonite. A government less driven by a desire for point-scoring would have understood that to call for a probe into the virus's origins barely two weeks after Wuhan emerged from its 76-day lockdown, when China had only recently buried some 4000 of its people, would not only provoke anger from the CCP but also cause genuine hurt and offence – even among Chinese citizens who had been agitating for transparency and accountability. Canberra directly challenged Xi Jinping at a moment of crisis. It was neither strategic nor a win for Australian soft power.

Neither was the McCarthyesque spectacle of Liberal senator Eric Abetz grilling Chinese Australians over their political loyalty in October 2020. The man who once opposed Section 18C of the *Racial Discrimination Act 1975* as an "affront" to free speech was now demanding that Chinese Australians express their criticisms of the

PRC in the precise terms he prescribed. Although he expressed outrage over China's treatment of Muslim Uighurs, would he welcome them as refugees, having previously called to prioritise Christians? The politician who referred to US Supreme Court justice Clarence Thomas as a "negro", consistently voted against the expansion of Aboriginal land rights and opposed the bill for marriage equality was playing the human rights champion. To paraphrase something Kevin Rudd said on *7.30*: what's needed is less attitude, more strategy. What exactly is the endgame envisioned by the "China hawks"?

To imply that if you are not in goosestep with the new Cold Warriors then you must be marching to Beijing's tune is self-defeating. How better, after all, to convince Australia's large and diverse Chinese Australian community that they will always be seen as outsiders, and suspect ones at that? If Beijing's propagandists had a sense of humour they would nominate Abetz for an award for services to the United Front.

I asked Richard McGregor of the Lowy Institute for his advice to the Australian government on China. He replied:

It can be boiled down to four words: Do more, say less. There is no nice way of pushing back against China and the CCP, and whatever you do is likely to come with a cost. But there is no need to make ourselves an easy target for Chinese sanctions, and I fear that's what the high-decibel mix of domestic and foreign policy has been doing of late.

It's worth remembering that Gough Whitlam normalised relations with China in the 1970s despite even starker differences in political ideology and economic systems than exist today. This decision has served us well for the best part of fifty years. The PRC is militarily and economically more powerful now, and Xi, like Mao before him, is a tough customer. But as the maintenance of plausible deniability around sanctions demonstrates, the PRC doesn't necessarily want to make an enemy of Australia any more than Australia should want to make an enemy of it.

"Did Xi just save the world?"

The cascade of bad tidings last year built to such a deafening roar that one piece of genuinely excellent news struggled to secure the attention it deserved. In a videolink address to the United Nations in September – the hottest September on record globally – Xi announced that China aimed to achieve carbon neutrality by 2060, with carbon dioxide emissions peaking by 2030.

The devil, as always, will be in the detail – to be revealed in March 2021, as part of the country's 2021–2025 Five-Year Plan – and in the execution. China is the single largest emitter of carbon dioxide, producing some 28 per cent of the world's total carbon emissions. To reach these goals, the PRC will need to invest some US$5 trillion in renewables, retrofit its coal-fired power plants with carbon capture and storage technology, and make major adjustments to manufacturing and transport.

It also has to deal with the consequences of a 2014 commitment to hand decision-making on coal-fired power to the provinces. The central government later introduced oversight to curb the predictable environmental damage and fiscal irresponsibility that resulted. But in early 2020, faced with a pandemic-related economic slowdown, it relaxed these restrictions, and the provinces quickly put 98 gigawatts of coal-fired power plants into construction – comparable, as researcher Jorrit Gosens has written for the *China Story Yearbook 2020*, to the "entire operational capacity" of Germany's and Japan's coal-fired plants combined. There's a staggering 250 gigawatts in development, counting plants still in the planning stage. Given that coal accounts for about 58 per cent of China's energy consumption, getting to "peak carbon" by 2030 is a big challenge. On the other hand, when the CCP decides on a policy, it has the power to follow through.

Xi announced the plan to the United Nations, which suggests that it is part of his effort to recast the international narrative around the PRC, promoting it as a responsible global leader. The plan is also vital for domestic stability. Climate change is what political scientist Pichamon Yeophantong calls a "threat multiplier" for existing stressors, especially in environmentally and politically sensitive areas such as Tibet, Mongolia and Xinjiang. Air, water and soil pollution have long contributed to local outbreaks of social unrest in China more broadly. The challenges of implementation may be considerable, but as *Foreign Policy* asked in a recent headline on the story, "Did Xi Just Save the World?"

There is a broad and growing international coalition of economists, scientists, businesses, bankers, farmers, schoolchildren and policymakers who believe that the world needs saving, and urgently. The International Monetary Fund advocates a combination of green stimulus and carbon pricing to supercharge post-pandemic economic recovery and mitigate the climate crisis. The European Union prioritised climate action in its response to the pandemic, and Joe Biden has pledged to reach net zero emissions by 2050. In contrast, Morrison's wishy-washy climate commitments threaten to make Australia not so much outlier as outlaw.

The lesson of Trump is that the institutions of democracy are not invincible

Research by the Investor Group on Climate Change shows that if Australia were to adopt a goal of net zero emissions by 2050, the decision would "unlock" A\$63 billion in investment over the next five years and hundreds of billions of dollars by 2050. Australian company directors, small-businessowners and doctors are among those who support a renewable-powered economic recovery. In July 2020, the government approved the construction of what will be the world's largest solar power farm on a cattle station between Darwin and Alice Springs. It should generate 1500 jobs directly and 10,000 indirectly during the construction phase, and 350 permanent positions once in operation. Much of the workforce will be recruited from Aboriginal communities in the Northern Territory. The station will power much of the Territory – and supply Singapore with 20 per cent of its energy needs. Imagine the benefit to Australian standing and influence in the region were we to focus on more such projects. We would reduce our emissions and reliance on coal while expanding and diversifying exports – and generate countless gigawatts of regional soft power at the same time. It could be a salve to Australia's relationships in the South Pacific, where rising sea levels threaten cultures and livelihoods, and where there is frustration with Australia's failure to take the climate crisis seriously.

A commitment to achieve carbon neutrality by 2050 would, theoretically at least, open up fresh opportunities for cooperation with China as well, including in clean technology research and development, trade and investment. Given that Japan and South Korea have made similar commitments, it would also unlock further possibilities for regional cooperation. We lead the world in lithium production, which, along with copper and nickel, are essential to the construction of clean-energy infrastructure such as storage batteries. A "gas-led" recovery, as advised by the gas-led National COVID-19 Commission Advisory Board, leads nowhere but dead ends – economic, environmental and political.

Can Australia save itself?

In September 2020, Minister for Foreign Affairs Marise Payne, speaking at the United Nations, condemned the repression in Xinjiang and the erosion of Hong Kong's rights and freedoms. A Chinese spokesperson sneered in response, "If Australia does care about human rights, it should address its own human rights problems in the first place, namely, guarantee the rights of refugees, migrants and Indigenous people, close its offshore migrants [sic] detention centres" and better protect its people from bushfires. *Global Times* threw "widespread racial discrimination" into the mix. This is not an argument about equivalence. It's simply that it would be easier for Australia to command the moral high ground if it hadn't dug itself such a hole.

According to PwC's Australia's Citizen Survey 2020, popular trust in government institutions rose during the bushfires and the COVID-19 pandemic, from a low of 18 per cent in 2018 to 46 per cent in October 2020. That survey found that the transparency and responsiveness demonstrated by government during these crises were key reasons for this newfound trust – which was notably lower among both 18- to 24-year-olds (14 per cent) and culturally and linguistically diverse communities (9 per cent). But public trust is friable.

Corruption scandals, misappropriation of public funds, pork-barrelling, dodgy tenders, questionable land purchases and resistance to FOI requests undermines the basis of trust, and, if not addressed, may well see that hard-won trust squandered. It's not just trust that's at stake. The prosecution of whistleblowers, attempts to prohibit environmental advocacy by charities and non-profits, and police raids on media are among factors that led the CIVICUS Monitor of "civic space" to downgrade Australia's rating from "open" to "narrowed" in 2019–20. It's hard to imagine that in 1984, a Labor minister was stood down for not declaring a stuffed Paddington Bear in his luggage when returning from an overseas trip.

Consider this: what if Chinese or other foreign agents seeking to influence our politics and our democracy faced a system in which parties were required to report all donations, large and small, with complete information on their source, as they came in? What if there were a mandated period between retiring from politics and taking up employment with companies, such as Huawei, that have a connection with previous political briefs or foreign powers? What if there were a powerful Australian National Audit Office, an independent Productivity Commission, an empowered and clean Australian Securities and Investment Commission, a politically agnostic Administrative Appeals Tribunal, a federal Independent Commission Against Corruption with teeth, and a strong, independent and well-funded ABC – and a healthier, more diverse media landscape in general? Without radical transparency combined with strict accountability, we will never know who our politicians are meeting with or who might be pulling their strings – and who might be pulling the strings of the string-pullers. Australia's sovereignty is at stake, and unless we see such reforms, the government is culpable of its endangerment.

The existing laws around "foreign interference" are so poorly and vaguely drafted that, as scholar of Xinjiang and China studies David Brophy has written, Australians could find themselves treated like terrorists as a result of "very ordinary forms of political discussion and exchange".

The expanding security state is a danger to, not a means of protection for, democracy. The politicisation of security laws was evident in Peter Dutton's comments on Chinese journalists expelled in September 2020 as part of an operation against foreign influence: "If people are here as journalists, and they're reporting fairly on the news, then that's fine. But if they're here providing a slanted view to a particular community, then we have a concern with that."

The CCP influences Chinese-language media in Australia through the provision or withholding of advertising revenues, the supply of ready-to-print stories and media ownership. Alternatives to PRC-influenced Chinese media include the Falun Gong–linked *The Epoch Times*, which runs a virulently anti-communist, pro-Trumpian and far-right conspiracist line. A simple, non-political fix to the predominance of disinformation would be to increase funding to SBS so that it can better serve Chinese and other ethnic communities – not only by translating news, information and entertainment into target languages, but also by generating original content. Enabling SBS to hire more Chinese-language reporters, editors and crew to cover local and China-related news would help to counter CCP influence-mongering while bolstering the democratic institution of a free and independent media. This is one of the many good ideas for strengthening Australian democracy and community cohesion suggested by Yun Jiang – an Australian National University researcher and director of the Canberra-based China Policy Centre, and one of the Chinese Australians grilled by Abetz over her loyalties.

The best way to deal with an ideologically driven, economically powerful Chinese autocracy cannot be to move in a similar direction. The lesson of Trump is that the institutions of democracy are not invincible. If we are to rise to the challenges presented by global autocracy, they must be guarded and strengthened. The profound disruption caused by COVID-19 is also an opportunity to rebuild. A clean and transparent political system and – crucially – a return to bipartisanship on foreign affairs as well as issues such as the climate crisis, a diverse media and a robust and accessible tertiary education system are as important in equipping Australia to deal with China's rise as are bolstered diplomacy and defence capabilities.

Knowledge is a renewable power source. That includes recognising that so long as the US–Australia alliance is intact, Beijing will regard Canberra – whichever party is in power – as America's lapdog. Strengthening regional alliances and engagement, including with the PRC, will help diffuse the impression that Washington says jump and Canberra asks how high.

We will never satisfy the CCP's demands of us. Nor should we strive to when they are unreasonable or offensive. But we must also work to understand where constructive cooperation is possible without compromising our principles or the integrity of our political system. We need to comprehend the extent to which these principles are threatened from within. The most potent superpower of a middle power is to be the best democracy it can be. ■

THE FIX
Solving Australia's foreign affairs challenges

—

Huong Le Thu on How Australia Can Supercharge Its Digital Engagement with South-East Asia

"Digital, technology and science capabilities are critical for the longer-term post-COVID recovery. In helping to fund them across South-East Asia, Australia will forge durable economic ties with partners in the region."

THE PROBLEM: As competition between the United States and China intensifies, South-East Asia is becoming the key competitive arena. Australia's engagement with the region is not only a matter of being a good neighbour, but a strategic imperative.

In November 2020, the Morrison government announced more than $500 million to support Australia's South-East Asian neighbours in a wide range of development goals, including in infrastructure, maritime resources and public health. While the commitment is welcome, it is designed to provide immediate assistance – within a three-to-four-year timeframe – but it is far from meeting the long-term needs of this complex region of more than 670 million people. Canberra intends to "compete constructively" with other powers in the region, as the foreign minister, Marise Payne, declared in December 2020. But dollar-for-dollar competition is neither feasible nor desirable. Current spending in South-East Asia is a drop in the ocean compared to the $1.4 billion promised for the much smaller region of the Pacific islands for 2019–21. Limits to aid resources are likely to continue in the near future due to the economic fallout from the COVID-19 pandemic.

Despite a shrinking aid budget, Australia can make a valuable contribution if it invests smartly and generously in South-East Asia's future, and focuses on areas in which it has expertise and experience.

THE PROPOSAL: Australia's South-East Asia engagement should focus on building the region's digital capacity. Australia has already begun to do this through various agencies, but its support is mainly delivered through aid. With the trend of cuts to aid budgets, it will be a challenge for Australia to make an impact through aid alone. Instead, Australia should adopt a comprehensive and long-term strategy that would modernise its traditional diplomacy, and would effectively support the region's resilience to cyberattacks, address its immediate needs and invest in its growing potential. This should be a whole-of-government commitment, similar to the Pacific Step-up.

The strategy should include supplying computers and hardware, improving skills, and retraining and assisting the region's workforce to adapt to the technological revolution. Some action is already underway. For example, Australia's CSIRO (Commonwealth Scientific and Industrial Research Organisation), in partnership with the Department of Foreign Affairs and Trade, operates in Singapore, Vietnam and Indonesia to support training in science, biosecurity, technology and the digital economy. But this work needs to be increased, and should form part of an overarching policy.

The Australian government has already pursued a cyber engagement strategy that seeks to support an open, free and secure internet globally. As part of that, it has assisted the ASEAN states to familiarise themselves with the United Nations' cyber norms, and conducted cyber capacity-building workshops in South-East Asia. But these initiatives in the region remain small, not specifically designed to target South-East Asia, and involve only a limited group of policy elites. The government also introduced a Cyber Cooperation Program, which will provide $34 million in grants over seven years to help countries with cyber security, and promote online human rights, democracy and gender equality. It's a great start – but with ambitions to play a substantive role and provide viable options throughout the Pacific, South Asia and South-East Asia, there needs to be more resources. These initiatives should be significantly expanded to encompass grassroots training across all levels of education, including early digital education for young students, cyber literacy programs in rural and remote areas, and retraining of the workforce to adapt to new, post-pandemic job demands.

Australia was one of the first nations to appoint an Ambassador for Cyber Affairs (Tobias Feakin) and support the UN's development of universal cyber norms. But Australia should further support South-East Asian partners to improve their security standards and cyber norms and bridge the region's digital gap. And if the Australian government is interested in regional partners sharing its views on security, and on decisions such as its ban on Chinese firm Huawei from participating in its 5G rollout, there needs to be a much more equal level of cyber awareness among South-East Asian governments and societies. Australia can capitalise on its international strength and contribute to laying the foundations of that awareness. The government has also allocated A$1.5 million to support the Australian Strategic Policy Institute to host The Sydney Dialogue in 2021 – a new annual international summit focused on issues related to cyber and critical technology.

Australia is sharply increasing its investment in "digital diplomacy" – using new digital and social media platforms to promote the country's interests. This demonstrates Canberra's recognition of how technology shapes the future of nations, and the importance of the shifting nature of diplomacy and engagement in the region, but the nation's technological engagement must extend beyond digital communication.

WHY IT WILL WORK: The pandemic has accelerated the digital transformation across the globe. But digital capability and cyber maturity across South-East Asia is very uneven. Singapore, for example, is one of the world's most technologically advanced countries, while Laos and Myanmar lag far behind. At the same time, South-East Asia is one of the most dynamic regions in the world when it comes to adapting to technological change. Indonesia, Vietnam and Thailand are developing ecommerce markets and homes for some of the world's most energetic innovation hubs. This should inform and shape Canberra's strategic and commercial engagement with the region, and its approach to development aid. Australia can make a significant contribution in bridging gaps between different countries' digital capabilities. Its cyber capacity and resilience are among the world's top ten, according to the 2020 National Cyber Power Index compiled by Harvard University.

Yet the pandemic has further exposed and deepened digital divides within individual countries. For example, when lockdowns meant that schools closed, online teaching was only an option for those with access to computers and the internet. Children in rural, poorer or less connected places missed out on education – the very means to overcome poverty and limited opportunities. If not addressed, this has a potential to create a "COVID generation" that will have lost key education opportunities. Similarly, occupations were disrupted to varying degrees by the pandemic. South-East Asia has a strong informal service-based economy. The national lockdowns, and the tourism and business travel freezes, took away the livelihoods of many, particularly in the hospitality and services sectors. Australia could help to support efforts to retrain workers and teach them digital skills.

Digital, technology and science capabilities are critical for the longer-term post-COVID recovery. In helping to fund them across South-East Asia, Australia will forge durable economic ties with partners in the region – including countries such as Indonesia, Thailand and Vietnam, which are expected to surpass Australia's gross domestic product in a couple of decades. Australia's support should be considered an investment in future two-way development, rather than seen as one-way aid.

By marrying traditional aid with modern digital diplomacy, Australia can mitigate some of the effects of its development budget cuts. This strategy would harness the talents of the next generations of South-East Asians and extend the reach of Australian dollars by allocating them to an area where a true difference can be made. Australia could provide the region with what it really needs, and ensure long-term change. Early investment and involvement in South-East Asian digital growth is not charity; it is investing in Australia's own economic future.

THE RESPONSE: The Department of Foreign Affairs and Trade said it was promoting the growth of digital skills and connectivity in South-East Asia as part of its commitment to regional engagement and to supporting the COVID-19 recovery.

"Australia's contribution has enhanced our partners' ability to manage cybersecurity risks, strengthen cybercrime responses and take advantage of opportunities provided by digital trade," a spokesperson said. "We will continue to enhance Australia's strategic approach to cyber issues in South-East Asia and globally, and address critical technology priorities, which are increasingly vital to Australia's foreign policy and national interests."

The department said that Australia has spent A$34 million since 2016 on more than twenty initiatives to strengthen cyber resilience. A further A$13 million will support greater coordination between Australia and South-East Asian countries in international standards-setting bodies.

"Australia is also working with South-East Asian partners to manage the effects of technology uptake – which COVID-19 has emphasised – on their workforces," the spokesperson said. "Australia and South-East Asia have a shared interest in an open, inclusive and resilient region, not least in ensuring a smooth recovery from COVID-19. South-East Asia's prosperity is our prosperity."

Reviews

Our Bodies, Their Battlefield: What War Does to Women
Christina Lamb
HarperCollins

I t is August 2018, and I am sitting with a reporter in a dark, hot room in the Kasaï region of the Democratic Republic of the Congo. It all feels like a tragic déjà vu. It has been almost ten years since I was last in the DRC. This time, we are on the other side of the country, in another conflict, covering the same issue – rape and sexual slavery is being used as a weapon of war.

A window in the room illuminates each woman as she tells her story. Some are pregnant or holding a baby. Defiant, brave, tired and far from the world's attention,

each of the women – Kabadi, Njiba, Marcelina, Elise, Vero, Bibisha, Monique, Monika, Tshilanda, Jose and Helene – walks us through the day she was raped and enslaved by armed men or boys, and how she eventually escaped or was released.

Kabadi Tshibuabua, who is from the Luba tribe, is nursing her baby daughter Philo on her knee – Philo was conceived in captivity. On a Sunday morning in April 2017, the Bana Mura militia came to Kabadi's village. She tells us how they fled the killing, along with hundreds of other people from her village, Cinq. She grabbed her two children – Beya, her three-year-old son, and Ntumba, her five-year-old daughter. As they ran into the bush, the militiamen, including teenagers, chased them. Ntumba was too slow and was captured on the banks of the river, where the militia murdered her with machetes. Kabadi had no choice but to keep running, to try to save Beya. She made it to a nearby village, not realising it was already under Bana Mura control. On the day she arrived, she was raped by five men, the last a militiaman by the name of Mowaja Rasta.

For a harrowing hour, the villagers gathered to deliberate over whether to sacrifice Kabadi and Beya. Rasta argued against it, for he wanted her as a second wife. Kabadi became a sex slave in his house. She fell pregnant in the second month of her captivity. The village chief, on a whim, released her after three months.

A year later, she and her two children are staying in a church in Tshikapa, the provincial capital, where she is eking out a living. We are told they are three of the lucky sixty-four who were released or escaped. Another ninety-three women and children are still being held in captivity. We listen to Kabadi's account. And then another woman enters the room, with a new account of horror.

It is brave women like this telling their stories whom you will meet in *Our Bodies, Their Battlefield* – a book that should be compulsory reading. In its pages, women who have endured the unimaginable speak out about what has happened to them and talk of their unwavering commitment for an acknowledgement of these war crimes and for a measure of justice.

One of the world's leading foreign correspondents, Christina Lamb has reported on war for decades for *The Sunday Times*, exposing atrocities and the impact on civilians. She continues to do so with a dedication to telling people's stories, and maintaining their dignity, that is not just inspiring but critical. Journalists like Lamb are doing vital work in documenting what happens in our world, in the hope that one day this preventable violence will stop.

Silence has often been history's approach to women. In *Our Bodies, Their Battlefield*, Lamb takes us into the lives of those who have survived rape across four continents and seventy years of conflict, places in which no woman is exempt from the threat of sexual violence.

In 1943, Japanese soldiers came to Lola Narcisa's village in the Philippines, forcing her into sexual slavery. She became one of the so-called "comfort women". Now eighty-seven, she tells Lamb:

> Until my last breath, I will shout to the whole world what they did to us. I still feel the pain. If only the Japanese government would just recognise and admit what they did to us. Whenever I hear on the news about women being raped, I get very angry.

Why are these things still happening to the Yazidis and others? Until we get justice, it will keep happening.

And justice is rare. As Lamb points out, the ISIS members currently on trial at Nineveh in northern Iraq all face the same charge: terrorism, which in Iraq carries the death penalty. But despite the countless testimonies of survivors and witnesses, the first rape or abduction charge was not laid until March 2020, after Lamb's book went to print. As Judge Jamal Dad Sinjari explains to Lamb when she asks why had no one been charged with keeping sex slaves or rape: "When these terrorists join ISIS, they are killing, raping, beheading, so it all counts as terrorism. That carries the death penalty, so there is no need to worry about the rape."

Lamb reminds us, again and again, why the women she spent time with – and the many more like them – need justice. The Tutsi sisters – Victoire Mukambanda and Serafina Mukakinani, known as Witness JJ and Witness NN – gave evidence at the International Criminal Tribunal for Rwanda trial in Arusha, Tanzania, that led to the world's first conviction for rape as a war crime. Victoire explains to Lamb how family and friends tried to put her off, "but in the end I decided that for justice to take place someone had to say what had happened and tell the world, and I was prepared to do it so these people would be punished and this wouldn't ever happen again".

Those of us who cover war and its aftermath sometimes have the distinct feeling that we are recording testimonies not only of war, but of war crimes. In the absence of a functioning justice system, sometimes we are the only ones who will listen when people report what has happened to them. I agree with Lamb and those at the many NGOs at work in this area that more needs to be done to allow women, their families and those children born in captivity access to the legal system, physical and mental health care, and economic support to rebuild their lives.

In South Sudan in 2016, during the peace negotiations to end the civil war, I met a baby called Dakhoa, meaning "destruction of the world". His mother, Chol, had fled the fighting and sought shelter at a United Nations camp for displaced peoples, where she still lives. During a lull in the conflict, Chol had gone home to retrieve her buried money, and on her way back to the camp was found by a group of government soldiers. "Some said, 'We have to rape her.' Some said, 'No, what is rape? We have to kill her,'" she told us.

Three of the soldiers raped her, while the others fought over her money. Dakhoa, sitting in his mother's lap, was conceived in this attack. Chol's husband, a rebel fighter, was in the bush and didn't know about the child. She still didn't know if he would acknowledge what happened to her as a crime or accept Dakhoa. In the meantime, she said, "We just survive."

A similar scene played out for us in Syria and northern Iraq under the brutal ISIS regime. During a visit to northern Iraq in 2019, several girls told us that they had witnessed mass killings and were forced into sexual slavery. Many were sold several times before being smuggled out or set free when the caliphate fell in March 2019. When battles are won or peace deals brokered, much attention is given to rebuilding – be it infrastructure or the economy – but the ordeal that women face continues. Their bodies may heal, but what has been taken from them cannot be restored. In many communities around the world, women who have been forced into sexual slavery and had children in captivity are shunned. An edict by the spiritual leader of the Yazidi declared that the Yazidi girls would be welcomed home, but the babies would not, for they had been fathered by ISIS. I know of two orphanages – one in Syria and one in Iraq – that care for these children. The children, like their mothers, will need support.

Lamb's book raises many questions that, after reading, swirled in my head for days. But one kept returning: why aren't war crimes against women talked about? My grandparents were German, and we grew up listening to the horrors of World War II, but I never heard them speak of these crimes. At school, we learnt of those killed in battles during both world wars – Gallipoli, Pearl Harbor, Normandy. We learn about the atrocities of genocide and ethnic cleansing, the Holocaust, prisoner-of-war camps such as Changi; we learn about politicians and generals, treaties and peace deals. Why not rape used as a weapon of war? I learnt about the comfort stations and women enslaved by the Japanese from a brief scene in the 1997 movie *Paradise Road*.

These war crimes must be included in history books. If we are mature enough to learn about mass killing and torture in high school, we should include the history of war crimes against women. It is a question of respect.

The outrage felt when reading Lamb's book – about the crimes, and about the failure of meaningful convictions, and about the continued practices of rape and sexual slavery – is galvanising. Yet alongside the darkness of humankind, Lamb also introduces us to survivors, family members and activists whose determination for justice is inspiring. We meet "unexpected heroes" who put their lives in danger to help. One is Nobel Peace Prize laureate Denis Mukwege, also known as Doctor Miracle, a gynaecologist in the Democratic Republic of the Congo who has treated more rape victims than anyone on Earth. Despite several threats on his life, for decades he has treated survivors, including babies. We also learn about the incredible risks Abdullah Shrim, a beekeeper and trader, took to rescue 367 women and girls from ISIS. "And when ISIS came and killed and stole our women, I decided to do something," he said. He persisted despite death threats: "My life is not more important than the tears of my niece or the other girls I have liberated."

Lamb also probes why armed groups throughout history commit these crimes. We hear from those who work with survivors as they try to explain the motives behind the madness – to humiliate, as a form of ethnic cleansing, as punishment. It rings true to me.

In 2009, I was sitting with a reporter in another dark, hot room, this time in Goma, the capital of North Kivu province in the Democratic Republic of the Congo. There was one window, which illuminated a wooden chair. The account was not from one of the many women who have sat before us for hours and talked us through the worst days of their lives. It came from a former child soldier, Augustin. He estimated that in the six months he fought with a militia, he raped eighty women. As far as we know, he has never been charged for his crimes. He remains a free man.

"Our leaders would force us to rape, to humiliate them, our adversaries," he said.

In almost a whisper, he describes how he raped so many

women. "First I would rape alone, and then I would rape in a group. I looked at the older ones doing it, and I did it too ... We would discuss it in a group, and we were proud to downgrade those girls. It was a matter of tribes, Mai Mai against Hutus ... We used to come to the villages, burn the houses and rape the women of our adversaries. When I think about it now, I feel very, very bad."

Augustin now holds talks with other men, aimed at discouraging rape. "I would like to ask forgiveness, but I don't know how to reach all of them, so my way of asking forgiveness is talking about it."

For many of the women survivors of this man-made plague, forgiveness is the last thing on their minds. Victoire – who Lamb describes pointing out the homes in the Rwandan village of Taba where Tutsi families were killed by Hutus – says of the banana tree groves on the hills, "I died so many times in those banana trees. I prayed to God to die."

Zamunda, whom I met in the Democratic Republic of the Congo in 2009, and whose husband and children were killed moments before she was shot in the genitals by militia, simply told me, "I wish sometimes the soldiers had killed me. I don't have anywhere to go, and no one to care for me." The main reason women like Zamunda, and the Luba women in the Kasai region, were coming forward was to tell the world that there were still women and children being held in captivity by the Bana Mura militia.

We need more female reporters and photographers like Lamb to report not only on conflict but also its aftermath, and to allow the women to speak for themselves. This is not an easy book to read, but it is a vital record, part of the project to change how women are treated in conflict, achieve justice for those who have suffered and hold those who commit these war crimes to account. Women should never be residual victims of war. There can be no more excuses.

Kate Geraghty

In the Dragon's Shadow:
Southeast Asia in the
Chinese century
Sebastian Strangio
Yale University Press

n November 2012, Barack
Obama was about to make
history as the first sitting
president to visit Cambodia,
the country the United States
had once secretly bombed as part
of the Vietnam War. Shortly before
his arrival, two large banners could
be seen hanging outside the East
Asia Summit venue in Phnom Penh.
"Long Live the People's Republic of
China," they proclaimed.

As far as diplomatic snubs go,
this one was less than subtle.

The Obama administration was
in the midst of its "pivot" to Asia to
counter the rising power of China.
Cambodia's prime minister, Hun Sen,
was making clear whose side he was on.

I covered the summit for the
ABC and remember feeling relieved
that there was actually a decent story,
given the mind-numbing dullness of
many regional forums.

A few months earlier, the Association of Southeast Asian Nations
(ASEAN) summit had imploded
when Cambodia that year, chair of
the regional bloc – vetoed even a mild
reference to China's territorial grab
in the South China Sea. For the first
time in its history, the summit failed
to issue a joint statement. In ASEAN
terms, this was epic.

After all those years of "no strings
attached" Chinese financing, the
patient puppeteer had finally yanked.
And Cambodia dutifully kicked.

Recounting the episode in
his new book, Sebastian Strangio
notes, "A few weeks earlier, Chinese
President Hu Jintao had visited
Phnom Penh, promising millions of
dollars in investment and assistance."

Strangio has a keen eye for
moments like these – the nubs of
history, where the money and power
plays and symbolism are revealed,
if only for an instant.

The Australian journalist
spent eight years based in Cambodia
(we both worked for *The Phnom Penh
Post*, although at different times)

and moved to Chiang Mai to finish writing *In the Dragon's Shadow*.

Covering nine countries, it is a serious and rewarding account of China's history, influence and possible future in South-East Asia, with little treasures scattered throughout, such as: "So far, ASEAN's preferred approach has been to bind the Chinese Gulliver with a thousand multilateral threads ... [of] the bloc's signature mode of sometimes glacial consensus-based diplomacy. It is an approach that amounts to a sort of narcotization by summitry."

Thinking back to the lows and highs of my ASEAN reporting experiences, desperately seeking anything even remotely newsworthy, that certainly resonates.

From the ritual kowtows before ancient emperors to the cash injections following the 1997 Asian financial crisis, Strangio does an admirable job of distilling centuries of history into a manageable primer. Two of the big themes of the book are the impacts of China's showpiece Belt and Road Initiative (BRI), and the role that South-East Asians of Chinese descent have played and might play in the future. "As in the US and Australia, where the CCP's wooing of diaspora communities has been the subject

of recent alarm, state efforts have extended beyond cultural outreach, seeking to convert Chinese cultural affinities into sympathy for [China's] state policies and support for official schemes like the BRI," he writes.

China's actions sometimes undercut its efforts to woo, Strangio points out, leading to a diplomatic strategy that ends up "less charm and more offensive".

Despite these quotable zingers, Strangio is most definitely not joining the chorus of critics taking pot shots at Beijing. I sense a writer genuinely trying to understand the motivations of China and each of its southern partners, and to fairly portray their actions. And if China's words and actions go awry sometimes, or appear contradictory – well, that's in the book too.

Some of those contradictions are captured by what the military strategist Edward Luttwak calls "great state autism". It's an apt phrase that pops up throughout the text. As this is a book primarily about China's impact on the world, most examples are of Beijing's "tin-ear for public opinion" or presumptions of superiority when dealing with smaller nations. But for balance, there's an acknowledgement that the

United States also has "a tendency to view the region's political developments through the lens of its own sense of exceptionalism . . . [believing] the American way is 'the ultimate destination of humankind'". As the uptake of authoritarianism in Cambodia and Thailand shows, many ASEAN states are quite partial to the Chinese model.

Conversations about the power struggle between the region's two superpowers – the United States and China – often cast South-East Asian nations as passive. While they may exist in the economic umbra of the dragon to the north, Strangio gives them agency and a backstory. Each country gets its own chapter – apart from Cambodia and Laos, which are sensibly grouped together, and East Timor and Brunei, which Strangio says were regrettably omitted due to time and space. These distinct national flavours are distilled into evocative chapter subheadings such as "Bamboo in the Wind" (Thailand), "Slouching Toward Beijing" (Philippines) and "Phobos and Deimos" for Cambodia and Laos. That last one is multi-layered. Like the two moons of Mars, Cambodia and Laos may indeed be small satellites "being drawn into close orbit around the red planet",

but Strangio leaves it to the reader to discover that Phobos and Deimos are also the twin Greek gods of fear.

The chapter on Singapore provides the scope to analyse China's maritime ambitions, a crucial element in Beijing's rise. Strangio describes how the legendary Chinese Muslim eunuch Admiral Zheng He is being revived as "the official mascot of China's new march to the sea", a peaceful alternative to the rapacious fleets of European colonisers. But he also notes historian Geoff Wade's caution that Zheng He's imperial armada wasn't as peaceful as is often made out.

This maritime theme is returned to in the chapter on the Philippines. Here, Strangio gives us the potent image of a solitary group of Filipino marines posted to a makeshift base fashioned from a rusting grounded ship, facing off against the freshly concreted island fortresses China has built nearby, troops, missiles and 3000-metre runways at the ready. The wild lurching of foreign policy under President Rodrigo Duterte is noted, but there's also an effort to see beyond the spectacle, to try to understand the wobbly, sometimes sweary balancing act between China and the United States.

Strangio offers insights from his interviews with prominent South-East Asian thinkers, as well as the occasional 'pub test': the views of market sellers and social media users, incensed at ill-mannered Chinese tourists or migrants. It is refreshing to see the region covered with clarity and nuance – not always common bedfellows.

For any reporter, diplomat, aid worker or businessperson heading to South-East Asia for the first time, *In the Dragon's Shadow* is a new entry on the "must-read" list. For those already entranced, it should become a well-thumbed reference of ideas, dates, quotes and further reading.

Liam Cochrane

China's Grand Strategy and Australia's Future in the New Global Order
Geoff Raby
Melbourne University Press

On the question of how to deal with China, Australia is a house divided. Those in one camp believe that China is a threat to Australia and must be confronted. Some in this camp feel that China will seek to impose regional and global hegemony, as the United States did after World War II; others fear not global dominance, but the insidious threat stemming from the ideology of the Communist Party of China, the authoritarian proclivities of Xi Jinping and/or the expanding Chinese military. Those in the other camp believe we should engage with China. Several argue that China faces internal challenges and global interdependencies that limit its ambitions and capabilities; others regard China's rise as inexorable and deserving of accommodation, rather than resistance.

Advocates of confrontation with China accuse their opponents of naivety and appeasement. In turn, proponents of engagement assert that strategies to push back against China, such as economic decoupling and aggressive rhetoric, risk dire financial consequences and fuel anti-Asian racism. These divisions on China policy have surfaced in political parties, the bureaucracy, the business world, the academy and think tanks, and sometimes play out in nasty ways on social media.

In general, those with inclinations towards security and defence lean towards confrontation while those of an economics and business bent favour engagement, though there are exceptions. For instance, the former head of Defence and the Australian Security and Intelligence Organisation (ASIO), Dennis Richardson, recently warned against the Australian Strategic Policy Institute's push to prioritise a national security agenda over economic needs.

Former ambassador to China Geoff Raby falls squarely in the engagement camp. In his new book, an important contribution to the "China debate", Raby argues that the threat of China has been overstated. China's ambitions remain limited to ensuring its territorial integrity, securing its borders and vital sea lanes, and maintaining the domestic dominance of the CCP. It lacks the brand of exceptionalism that has driven other rising powers, and it will not attempt to marginalise its regional rivals, Japan and the United States, because they are too strong, and too useful.

Raby unfurls this argument across three chapters, peppered with insights from his time as a diplomat and an ambassador. Not only is China's "grand strategy" not so grand, he argues, but Beijing will struggle to achieve even its limited goals. Unlike the United States during its rise to power, China has a fraught history and geography that has left it in ongoing territorial disputes with countries including India, Japan and Vietnam, and it faces challenges over Taiwan, Hong Kong, Tibet and Xinjiang. Its efforts to exercise soft power internationally through influence and interference have been largely unsuccessful, and have invited a backlash. What's more, China's economic model has resulted in a heavy dependence on imported resources.

The Belt and Road Initiative (BRI), and institutions such as the Shanghai Cooperation Organisation, the Asian Infrastructure Investment Bank and the New Development

Bank, are often mooted as evidence of China's plan to construct an alternative regional order, but Raby argues they instead constitute a parallel "bounded order". This order intersects with and sits alongside existing multilateral institutions, in which China often behaves as a status quo power. Moreover, Raby notes, the BRI and aid outreach to resource-rich countries has often overpromised and underdelivered. Indeed, China's recent focus on a "dual circulation" strategy, which places greater emphasis on domestic consumption and supply chains, may in part be driven by mounting problems with BRI projects, which have been exacerbated by the COVID-19 pandemic and slowing global economic growth.

Raby points out that Australia has often got China wrong. He attributes Canberra's recent confrontational stance to policy-makers' lack of understanding of China's constraints and ambitions and to a historical "fear of abandonment" by bigger Western powers. By yoking to the United States, and cultivating the Quad (Australia, Japan, the United States and India) and the rhetoric of the Indo-Pacific as mechanisms for balancing and containing China's influence, Australia has become a proxy strategic competitor to China without a coherent plan to maintain the mutually beneficial economic relationship. To this end, Raby proposes a new grand strategy for Australia, based on the promotion of a more independent foreign policy aimed at maintaining stability in East Asia and engaging China.

However, his policy prescriptions are underwhelming. Raby urges a return to a middle-power diplomatic agenda in the Asia-Pacific, citing Australia's promotion of the Asia Pacific Economic Community in the 1980s. He recommends a strategy of hedging through close involvement in the Association of Southeast Asian Nations (ASEAN). He also touts the maintenance of the security relationship with the United States, albeit with increased defence spending in anticipation of Washington's declining reliability, and a continued economic partnership with China, combined with greater cooperation.

Australian officials might respond that much of this is already taking place. For example, the recently concluded Regional Comprehensive

Economic Partnership agreement, which is curiously ignored in the book, was championed by Australia, Japan and ASEAN, and integrates China into a fifteen-nation trade framework. The Morrison government has lately declared that it intends to pursue a policy of strategic patience with China. But Raby goes further, suggesting Canberra seek a formal association with the BRI and Chinese entry into the Quad, two developments that are unlikely to occur. He also points out that Australia's criticisms of China's behaviour, though legitimate, are often expressed loudly and stridently, with little effect aside from a continued deterioration of the relationship.

Among the challenges Raby foresees for Australia, in developing a close involvement in ASEAN, is the need to work with governments with poor democratic and human rights records. Here Raby need not worry, for Australia has never had much trouble accommodating authoritarian regimes. Recall that in 1989, the same year that foreign minister Gareth Evans advanced "good international citizenship" as a pillar of Australian foreign policy, he was photographed drinking champagne with Ali Alatas, foreign minister in the Indonesian Suharto dictatorship, to celebrate a deal to divvy up the oil and gas reserves of East Timor – a territory Jakarta had annexed and ruled through brutal repression. Today, the Morrison government hails its "shared values" with the autocratic regime that rules Vietnam and the increasingly authoritarian government of India – Australian policy-makers' fear of China has already had the effect of reducing values to little more than the defence of state sovereignty. Moreover, the slow erosion of civil liberties in Australia, through legislation such as the *ASIO Amendment (Terrorism) Act 2003* and the *ASIO Amendment Bill 2020* – the latter a direct response to concerns about Chinese interference – means that Australia has moved closer to its neighbours in the past two decades when it comes to the assertion of state power over citizens.

Ultimately, a truly independent foreign policy would require Australia to move away from both dependence on the United States for its security and on China for its economy. The abandonment of the US–Australia alliance and reducing our reliance on resources exports to China would undoubtedly be too radical for Raby. But the United States is showing obvious signs of decline, and China is now indicating a desire to reduce its foreign economic dependence. The price of "alliance maintenance" has been laid bare in the Brereton Report on Australian war crimes in Afghanistan.

The economic importance of resource exports to Australia has led to an unwillingness to address climate change, despite its deleterious effects regularly on display during Australia's long, hot summers. The time may have come for the staid field of Australian foreign policy to consider some radical options.

Priya Chacko

Not Always Diplomatic:
An Australian Woman's
Journey through
International Affairs
Sue Boyd
UWA Publishing

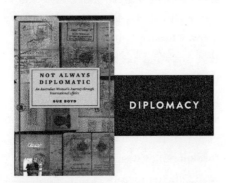

Why has the profession of diplomacy suffered a loss of prestige over recent decades? There are many

explanations, but one reason is simple: too few citizens understand what it is that diplomats actually do.

This makes *Not Always Diplomatic*, a memoir by one of Australia's first female ambassadors, particularly welcome. Sue Boyd has served during interesting times, as the saying goes, from Portugal's Carnation Revolution and Cold War East Germany to nuclear weapons negotiations at the United Nations headquarters in New York. In the region, she's been head of mission in developing Bangladesh, tiger economy Vietnam, post-handover Hong Kong and coup-era Fiji.

Kim Beazley launched this book and described it as a "rollicking good yarn" in his foreword. I worked with Sue Boyd at the Australian

Institute of International Affairs, and reading this is a lot like sharing a meal with her as she regales you with stories of distant places and times (being a good raconteur is a key skill of diplomacy). She takes the reader through the warp and weft of diplomatic life, providing a "view from the trenches", having served under twelve foreign ministers between 1970 and 2003. She also offers intriguing snippets of diplomatic tradecraft – and gives a sense of the valuable work diplomats do.

A diplomat's job, Boyd observes, focuses on three questions. As Gough Whitlam put it when he called on her to brief him on Portugal and Timor: "What's going on? What does it mean for Australia? And what should we do about it?"

When a diplomat is dropped into a new posting, the task is to try to understand the workings of the country, identify Australia's interests and advance them. This involves developing a deep understanding of the country's motivations, and building relationships with the people that matter. Boyd gives example after example of how she cultivated connections in what is famously a "people profession".

There is plenty of grist for those who are distrustful of elites. She mentions meetings with royalty. And learning golf. I doubt she'd be apologetic. Getting into the minds of influential people is a vital part of a diplomat's work.

One reason that diplomacy is the key institution of international society, as international relations theorist Hedley Bull described, is that intercultural understanding is very difficult. This is underappreciated in an age when news flows instantly around the world, giving us events but not deep understanding. In his foreword to the book, Beazley writes, "Those who say all we need to know is in the public arena in various forms of media could not be more wrong."

Spanning thirty-four years, *Not Always Diplomatic* charts many changes in the status and practice of diplomacy. For instance, communications underwent a revolution during Boyd's career. When she started, the department had one huge computer and a typing pool. She sent messages via telex (an explanation is provided for younger readers). In East Germany, she rightly assumed she would be surveilled and her phone conversations recorded, but she didn't have to worry about cyber threats. When she was the foreign affairs spokesperson during Iraq's invasion of Kuwait, she would appear on breakfast television, but she didn't have to contend with the 24-hour news cycle. By the end of her career, the ready availability of information on international events, as well as the ease of travel, had undermined diplomats' status as a privileged source of knowledge.

Boyd makes a compelling case that today there is still the need for skilled teams on the ground, with the right contacts, a detailed understanding of what is going on, resources and nous, and the capacity to "find the right path". She gives an example of this – her time in Fiji during the 2000 coup, led by George Speight – that comprehensively debunks the fashionable idea that diplomats are less essential than those from a military background in safeguarding Australia's security. During the 56-day crisis, she, as high commissioner, was commanding officer for all diplomatic staff, ensuring their safety and that of other Australians on the ground. She played a vital role in helping to broker an agreement among the parties,

made possible by her deep personal relationships. This is national security by diplomatic means.

Not Always Diplomatic also offers a valuable description of the process of promoting diversity within an organisation. Boyd's career coincided with massive change for women in foreign affairs. When she joined DFAT, she was one of only two women in the graduate intake, and was paid 10 per cent less than male colleagues for the same work. The marriage bar – which required women to resign from the public service upon marriage – meant that there was a reluctance to hire women, and so almost no role models for Boyd. She characterises the department as a "sexist minefield of low expectations, resistance, hostility". There were lewd comments. Additional hospitality responsibilities. Exclusion from particular posts. She was conscious of being judged not just as a diplomat, but as a woman diplomat.

She describes weaving gently through this environment, to carve out a better workplace: "We danced the constant dance of upsetting the men as little as possible so that they became allies rather than adversaries."

How Boyd worked with others to enable better conditions for women offers valuable lessons for those who are trailblazers in their professions, whatever "non-traditional" group they belong to. These lessons include using your skills to your advantage, learning the importance of mentors and champions, being proactive in your career progression, overcoming impostor syndrome and not discounting your own competence.

Boyd broke a glass ceiling to become Australia's first female ambassador to an Islamic country when she was posted to Bangladesh in 1986. She stayed in the diplomatic service long enough to see it welcome rather than tolerate women. In 2017, Frances Adamson, the first female secretary of the Department of Foreign Affairs and Trade, said that Boyd had been a mentor to and role model for most of the women in the department.

Today, fifty years after Boyd entered the department, its funding is at the lowest percentage of the federal budget in our nation's history. As I wrote in a previous issue of this journal: the combined diplomacy, trade and aid budget was 8.9 per cent of the budget in 1949, compared to 1.3 per cent in 2019.

To raise awareness of this underfunding of Australia's diplomatic capacity and why it matters, we need more diplomats explaining their work. May they all share Boyd's humour, candour and pragmatism.

Melissa Conley Tyler

Correspondence

"Balancing Act"
by Rory Medcalf

Rikki Kersten

I n his essay on the Quadrilateral Security Dialogue (AFA10: *Friends, Allies and Enemies*), Rory Medcalf portrays the Quad as a minilateral grouping whose primary role is to counterbalance China in Asia and the Indo-Pacific. Medcalf describes the decisive part Japan's former prime minister Shinzō Abe played in facilitating a Quad comeback, and his Indo-Pacific activism, as "asserting Japan's strategic normality". In fact, Japan's evolving Indo-Pacific strategy is anything but normal. As the Quad develops more heft, Australia must fully appreciate the nature and extent of Japan's strategic ambition in the Indo-Pacific.

Quad 1.0 was grounded in the ideas articulated in Abe's speech to the Indian parliament in August 2007. There, Abe unveiled what was to become his foreign policy mantra during his second term in office (2012–20). The rhetoric of liberal internationalism dominated, with references to "the arc of freedom and prosperity" and the relationship between maritime security and democratic values. The situating of Japan–India defence cooperation in an Indo-Pacific region that stretched from the east coast of the United States to Africa, together with the notion of "maritime democracies", became integral to Abe's vision for an expanded role for Japan. Whether it was called the "arc", the "security diamond" or the "free and open Indo-Pacific" (as Abe's policy termed it), Abe was determined to project an image of Japan as a champion of liberal internationalism, and a protector of the "global commons".

Even in this first Quad, Japan's ambition to help contain China's behaviour was clear. It was not a matter of "balancing" so much as shaming. Abe wanted Japan to be regarded internationally as a more desirable and ethical partner than China, whether in security, trade, finance, aid or infrastructure development.

Abe's foreign policy vision also included Japan being a future rule-maker, instead of merely a rule-abider. The Expanded Partnership for Quality Infrastructure (EPQI) – a globally focused development scheme worth US$110 billion, conceived as a kind of counterweight to China's Belt and Road – was aimed at ensuring this. The plan, which Japan announced at the G7 summit it hosted in 2016, doesn't match the Belt and Road in dollar terms, but it utilises Japan's reputational advantage over China, forming coalitions of like-minded nations (such as the Blue Dot Initiative, comprising Japan, Australia and the United States) to ensure the quality, sustainability and transparency of infrastructure-related development assistance in Asia. To date, EPQI projects have included the Mumbai–Ahmedabad high-speed rail project in India, the North–South Commuter Railway project in the Philippines and the Asia–Africa Growth Corridor concept.

The striking aspect of Japan's Free and Open Indo-Pacific strategy – issued in 2016, and subsequently defined as a "vision" – was that it combined a geographically expanded foreign policy that encompassed the Indo-Pacific with a less constrained security stance. In this way, Japan's foreign policy activism became an enabler for its security policy. An important part of this approach is creating a successful defence equipment and technology export industry. Instead of having to hide behind the banner of assisting regional neighbours in the para-military sphere through the auspices of a defence aid program (such as donating patrol boats to the Philippines coast guard), the provision of military goods to regional nations for a military purpose indirectly serves to legitimise Japan's defence-related actions to both regional and domestic constituencies.

From this perspective, the reborn Quad is a perfect facilitator for Japan's enhanced ambitions. The Quad, especially the Quad-Plus variant that includes dialogues with Vietnam, South Korea and New Zealand, will assist Japan to normalise the export of defence equipment and technology to those countries that are – to quote Japan's 2015 security policy legislation – "in a close relationship with Japan". Japan's commitment to this approach was demonstrated by Prime Minister Yoshihide Suga's decision to make his first overseas visit to Vietnam. During this visit, in October 2020, Suga secured a deal to supply Japanese patrol planes and radar equipment to Vietnam. Japan has subtly shifted its rhetoric from an emphasis on "maritime democracies" to a "rules-based order" – a change specifically designed to enable it to work with regional partners such as

Vietnam, which do not fit so neatly into the "maritime democracies" category. It is no accident that respective statements issued after Quad 2.0 ministerial meetings likewise have featured rhetoric that is more inclusive. Japan's foreign minister, Toshimitsu Motegi, highlighted the agreement among Quad members on the importance of "broadening cooperation with more countries" to achieve peace and prosperity in the region after COVID-19; Australia's counterpart, Marise Payne, pointed to the need for stronger cooperation with regional partners and institutions, including in quality infrastructure investment; and India's external affairs minister, Subrahmanyam Jaishankar, referred to the "free, open and inclusive Indo-Pacific" as a place where enhanced connectivity and infrastructure development were a priority.

Before Abe's second term in office, "normal" for Japan would have meant avoiding defence and security activism, and limiting its global ambition to initiatives around climate change, international aid and disaster relief. Keeping the United States engaged in the defence of Japan and Asia would have meant focusing on sub-alliance networking, such as with Australia, rather than forging deep security relationships with non-US allies such as India and Vietnam.

But the evolution of the Quad, and Japan's foreign and security policy activism, signal that it is moving beyond a desire to be just a rule-keeper. Instead, it wants to be a key player in envisioning new multilateral arrangements in the Indo-Pacific that are not wholly dependent on United States leadership. This represents the new normal for Japanese security policy.

As Australia deepens its security relations with Japan, it should be mindful of this shift in Japan's ambition. Australia no longer needs to cajole a reluctant Japan to perform a more proactive security role in the region via the safe haven of a multilateral gathering. Rather, it has a like-minded partner in the Indo-Pacific that is willing to lead, and capable of leading, multilateral endeavours such as the Quad-Plus in the security sphere.

Rikki Kersten is a Canberra-based researcher and analyst,
and professor emerita at Murdoch University.

Pradeep Taneja

R ory Medcalf has long championed an enhanced security role for India in the geographical space, encapsulated by the concept of the Indo-Pacific. He is also an ardent advocate of a closer partnership between Australia and India. His understanding of the security dynamics of this region is second to none.

Medcalf's article on the Quad captures the origins, purpose and limitations of this security grouping very well. He sees strong merit in the alignment of security interests of the four countries that make up the Quad: Australia, Japan, India and the United States. He also does not hide the fact that the Quad has become a subset of the China policy of all four of these countries. I agree with his contention that the Quad is not the only solution to Australia's challenge of charting a strategic course through the troubled waters of the Indo-Pacific; that would indeed require a multi-layered approach, including building up Australia's own defence capabilities.

My purpose here is not to find fault with Medcalf's reasoning or to disagree with him on the functions and limitations of the Quad. Instead, I want to focus on why India has taken so long to feel comfortable sitting down with the other three to discuss security and, importantly, the challenges that China's increasing power and ambition present to the regional security order.

Firstly, the new minilateral form of security cooperation that the Quad embodies suits India better than bilateral or multilateral alliances involving formal security obligations. It is more in line with India's desire to maintain strategic autonomy and its newfound preference for multi-alignment. As Medcalf rightly points out, "India will not easily shake off its long allergy to alliance entanglements", but it is now more open to security cooperation with other nations, both big and small, than it has been since independence in 1947.

India has come a long way from the era of non-alignment and suspicion of the West. To be sure, there are still plenty of retired diplomats and intellectuals in New Delhi who warn against the dangers of growing security cooperation with the United States. But these days they are more likely to be found writing their own blogs or debating world affairs in club dining rooms than in the corridors of power.

Secondly, India is gradually shedding its fear of China and actively seeking to balance Chinese power, especially in South Asia and the Indian Ocean. While India remains cognisant of China's sensibilities, it is not willing to allow China a veto over its relations with other countries. Ironically, China's aggressive moves on the Line of Actual Control, the undefined border between the two Asian giants, over the past few years have freed India from any inhibitions it may have had about offending China.

Finally, India is catching up to China in border infrastructure. Long held back from building roads and bridges along its border with China by the fear that better road connectivity might work against it in the event of war, India has been building border infrastructure at a furious rate over the past decade or more. This has given it confidence, along with the deterrent capabilities it has developed, to seek security partnerships with like-minded countries without fearing reprisals from its more powerful neighbour.

Medcalf raises the question of how the Quad and other new blocs would engage with Beijing and the institutions initiated by China. India's experience can be useful here. It is a member of the China-initiated Asian Infrastructure Investment Bank and Shanghai Cooperation Organisation (SCO), as well as the Brazil–Russia–India–China–South Africa (BRICS) grouping. In other words, India's participation in the Quad has not stopped it from participating in other minilaterals with China. So far it has been able to walk on both sides of the street.

Some Indian scholars, such as Rajesh Rajagopalan, have questioned the viability and sustainability of India's parallel participation in the Indo-Pacific strategy and the Quad, both of which China regards as part of US efforts to contain its rise, and fora like the SCO, where China is the dominant influence. Prime Minister Narendra Modi is known, for example, to attend back-to-back trilateral meetings with the leaders of the United States and Japan on the one hand, and the presidents of Russia and China on the other, on the sidelines of the G20 summit.

Of course, India is not the only country trying to juggle its participation in China-led fora with its involvement in United States–led security dialogues. But India is the largest such power that is trying to devise complicated sets of policies to deal with China's rise. India's decision to invite Australia to the 2020 Malabar exercise, which also includes the United States and Japan, indicates its determination to remain a key member of the Quad while maintaining its foreign policy autonomy.

Pradeep Taneja is a senior lecturer in Asian politics and a fellow of the Australia India Institute at the University of Melbourne.

Rory Medcalf responds

My article was subtitled "Making Sense of the Quad" and it was intended to do just that. The Quadrilateral Security Dialogue involving India, Japan, Australia and the United States has often been misunderstood – sometimes wilfully, as with Chinese foreign minister Wang Yi's early 2018 claim that it was a passing fad which, along with the notion of the Indo-Pacific, would "dissipate like ocean foam". Well, here we are, three years on, and the idea of cooperation among Indo-Pacific partners to balance Chinese power, typified by the Quad, is going strong.

The foreign policy debate in Australia has come a long way in recent years, and recognition of the Quad's relevance and durability has fast become mainstream. It is good to see two of the nation's leading specialists on Japan and India, Professor Rikki Kersten and Dr Pradeep Taneja, complement my analysis with their fine-tuned explanations of why the Quad makes particular sense for those countries.

Kersten notes that Japan's evolving strategy of building coalitions to balance China – including via the Quad – is "anything but normal". I suspect we are ultimately in agreement here. My point that Tokyo's wider security activism in the Quad and elsewhere is about "asserting Japan's strategic normality" was a way of saying that Japan is now willing to play power politics, promote and protect its interests, and fight coercion with coalitions and deterrence, ending the self-abnegating era of its diplomacy.

Both correspondents rightly point out that Australian policy-makers need to be aware of the distinct national agenda of our Quad partners. I agree with Kersten that Australia needs to appreciate the nature and extent of Japan's strategic ambition in the region. My point is that such ambition is broadly congruent with Australia's interests and values. Neither country wants our region dominated by one power – a shared goal that underscores the strengthened Australia–Japan partnership. This was reflected in ministerial and prime ministerial meetings in late 2020 – including Scott Morrison's first overseas trip since the outbreak of the COVID-19 pandemic – and in new agreements spanning defence, technology and infrastructure.

Likewise, Taneja points out that India has its own motives. He shines a light on India's adroit diplomacy in strengthening the Quad, notably through inviting Australia back into the Malabar naval exercise in late 2020, as my article anticipated it would. At the same time, he notes India's ability to juggle other arrangements involving China, such as the Shanghai Cooperation Organisation and the China–Russia–India summit. I agree that New Delhi has good reason for seeking this kind of omnidirectional engagement: in a confusing and multipolar world, it's a nice thing to have. I am not so sure, however, that it is sustainable. We have just lived through a deeply consequential year, and for India the shock of 2020 extends beyond COVID-19 to include a brutal reassessment of its relations with China. Violence on a contested border has compounded Indian popular mistrust of China for years to come. No wonder India is intensifying its investment in a whole range of China-balancing partnerships, including the Quad. It's quite likely that India will increasingly privilege them over what is left of its China engagement, especially if its willingness to reject Chinese infrastructure (the Belt and Road Initiative) and technology ambitions (the entire suite of Chinese phone apps) is anything to go by.

Given Australia's own confronting year with China, we can expect that Canberra will have plenty of reason to advance its agenda of Indo-Pacific coalition-building in 2021, seeking safety in numbers. The question remains how supportive the various partners will be of one another as China keeps making the going tough. An Australian priority will be to ensure that the Biden administration recognises the Quad and the wider Indo-Pacific balancing strategy for what they are: authentically partner-driven initiatives that warrant sustained American support.

Rory Medcalf is a professor and head of the
National Security College at the Australian National University.

"Goodbye, America"
by Patrick Lawrence

Charles Edel

Patrick Lawrence's essay "Goodbye, America" (AFA10: *Friends, Allies and Enemies*) argues that America's focus on Asia is based on an obsolete understanding of regional dynamics and a nostalgic desire to prolong American primacy. Believing otherwise, Lawrence writes, is simply wishful thinking born out of "longing for the once-was, anxiety in the face of change and an appallingly poor grasp of China's aspirations and intentions". That assumption underlies the essay's conclusion that in the face of such US intransigence, Asia should just get on with the business of accommodating Beijing's interests.

To Lawrence, governments that oppose China are recklessly courting disaster, and mortgaging their national interest to a misguided and disengaged United States. He directs this critique towards several countries. Canberra, Wellington and Tokyo all come in for reproach for displaying variations of America's "frenzy of Sinophobia".

Lawrence goes further, arguing that China's rise has been peaceful, non-imperial, cooperative and supportive of multilateral efforts to resolve disputes. Any nation that does not understand this, in this rendering, misjudges the Chinese government and favours a distant United States whose interests "have never been congruent with anyone else's."

One country that does not make his list of reckless actors, however, is China. Curiously, for an essay that is premised on the need to better understand China, there is virtually no discussion of the rapid changes China has undergone, or of the actions it has taken to destabilise, coerce and intimidate virtually every single one of its neighbours.

Yet those changes and actions are key to understanding how nations view and are responding to a more repressive, powerful and aggressive China.

And yet, this essay ignores the domestic changes in China that have made it more challenging to conduct business on equal terms, have made China more repressive and have rendered it even less transparent. Actions that have compromised the sovereignty of multiple countries, sought to harm nations for decisions that do not privilege Beijing's expanding set of core interests and destabilised the region are either explained away or attributed to Washington's provocations. Nowhere in this essay is there a discussion of the dramatic changes Xi Jinping has unleashed in China, the confrontational foreign policy Beijing has embarked upon or the sense of alarm China has engendered worldwide.

China's activities before and during the coronavirus pandemic have resulted not only in sharper policy responses by other governments, but also in a significant hardening of public attitudes towards the Chinese government. For these reasons, an increasing number of nations, by no means just the United States, have undertaken a fundamental reassessment of how and on what terms to deal with Beijing.

Instead of acknowledging any of this, Lawrence echoes Beijing's talking points by attributing virtually all regional tensions to American provocations. In relation to the South China Sea – where China has occupied and militarised multiple island features, destroyed thousands of acres of coral reef, attacked fishers from multiple countries, ignored the international ruling deeming its claims excessive, interfered with the naval vessels of multiple nations, interrupted lawfully undertaken resource surveys, intimidated coast guards and delayed negotiating a code of conduct for more than a decade – the essay claims that "China seeks nothing more than a role in securing its neighbourhood".

Freedom-of-navigation operations, legal exercises that demonstrate the United States will not accede to maritime claims that violate international law, are dismissed as a "cynical ruse" that cut against the interests of South-East Asia. Lawrence reports, "I haven't noted any Malaysian, Filipinos, Vietnamese or Bruneians banging on the Pentagon's door asking for wandering warships to come their way". While those countries may have been cautious in their public response to violations of their maritime boundaries and harassment of their citizens and navies, the United States cooperates with each, operates from bases in two of them, and has regularly fielded their requests to deploy more US military assets to the region. As for the nascent quadrilateral grouping of Australia, Japan, India and the United States, Lawrence quotes China's foreign minister, Wang Yi, who dismissed the Quad as both a deliberate provocation against China and fundamentally unserious, to conclude that "the Pacific littoral will be much better off if events prove Wang right". No matter that the Quad has taken shape in response to China's use of military and economic coercion; this essay seems to imply that any steps taken in response to Beijing's actions are a provocation. Here, as elsewhere, Lawrence reverses cause and effect to portray China as an innocent and aggrieved party.

The insistence on attributing the region's tensions to Washington's actions ignores a crucial fact: that much of the United States' increasingly serious and bipartisan focus on Asia has been a reaction to Beijing's activities and the demands of America's allies and partners. What makes this essay so unconvincing, however, is that it fails to take into account that most Asian countries are seeking to balance the threat of an increasingly aggressive China. This is not a US-driven construct, but the reality faced by all of China's neighbours in the region.

An American presence in the Pacific is not a nostalgic relic, as Lawrence portrays it. The hub-and-spoke model of bilateral security relationships in Asia, as envisioned during the Cold War, was intended to deter aggression *against* allies and partners, and to moderate security competition among them. This provision of common security had the added benefit of setting the conditions for the Asian economic miracle. Today, a US presence ensures that the region is not subsumed by a Chinese sphere of influence which holds out the promise of economic benefit in exchange for political compliance. Countries, including Australia, have made a determination that such a future is manifestly not in their interests. This has resulted in deliberate policy choices by sovereign governments. It is not, as Lawrence argues, simply outsourcing their defence and their strategic thinking to Washington.

Indeed, the evidence Lawrence offers for the above assessment seems to be that Australia (and others) have chosen to resist China's encroachments into their internal affairs and its efforts at economic coercion, and strengthened their defence capabilities. In this, Lawrence falls for the most cynical of all Chinese talking points, ascribing the choices of independent nations not to their own agency, but to some kind of deferential and mindless subservience, as US allies. He neglects a more compelling argument – that Canberra and others have indeed been shaping a "new order" that is "expressive of the interests and aspirations of those creating it, and no one else's". After all, it just might be possible that multiple countries in Asia believe their aspirations remain theirs to define, and that their futures will be shaped by choices they make.

Charles Edel is a senior fellow at the United States Studies Centre at the University of Sydney and a global fellow at the Wilson Center.

Thom Dixon

P atrick Lawrence's essay is laced with questions, but perhaps none better than those raised by the title. Who is saying goodbye to America, and what kind of America are they farewelling? By Lawrence's account, neither Australia nor Japan wishes to farewell America. Instead, these two countries live in a state of nostalgic longing for an America that was and the pre-eminence it once had.

As I read Lawrence's essay, I was reminded of an event I attended at the Tunisian Embassy in Tokyo – a quaint building tucked away on a side street opposite the Yasukuni Shrine. All the Japanese Ministry of Foreign Affairs representatives I spoke to were concerned they couldn't match the growing Chinese infrastructure and development spend throughout North Africa and the Middle East. That was 2016, and a reminder that Australia's narrow focus on countering Chinese spending in the Pacific neglects the contest for influence across the Indo-Pacific and beyond.

Lawrence uses the term "Indo-Pacific" but once in the article, to refer to the renamed US Indo-Pacific Command. "Asia-Pacific" is used just as sparingly. This determined separation of Asia from the Pacific gives rise to the questions threaded through the essay, about how America and its allies view and define the Asia and Pacific regions. Lawrence asks if America ever returned to a peacetime posture since 1945, and he questions why Japan and Australia remain so heavily invested in the postwar order when there is so much to gain from "a new reading of their circumstances".

The answers to these questions depend on who and where the reader is, and what they stand to lose or gain from the changing geopolitical landscape.

Lawrence's essay is effective in illustrating the contest underway for control of narratives about the region. Try lining up the transcripts of speeches by China's foreign minister, Wang Yi, and America's former secretary of state Mike Pompeo, then reconcile their conflicting accounts of disputes in the South China Sea.

I had my lesson in post-truth politics at a non-proliferation workshop in New Zealand in 2017. Representatives of a think tank attached to the North Korean Ministry of Foreign Affairs were detailing their opinions on regional nuclear non-proliferation. Meanwhile, everyone else in the room was doom-scrolling Twitter as North Korean missiles flew over Japanese waters. These missiles were never mentioned during the two-day conference.

That workshop was funded by the US Department of Energy. Lawrence highlights the potential of such work in his statement that "diplomacy is twenty-first-century statecraft's defining technology". He also notes that in the immediate aftermath of 1945, when the hub-and-spokes model of the Asia-Pacific was dominant, the critical diplomatic manoeuvring was conducted in Washington. But the principal seat of diplomatic power in Asia is unlikely to remain in Washington forever. Indeed, the man who held that position until January 2021 defaced American democratic institutions and whittled away the symbols, authority and prestige that underpin American rhetoric and international action. Though these institutions have displayed resilience, it is difficult to estimate the long-term damage.

Who controls the treadles of diplomacy in Asia now? Who wields power over truth? "Goodbye, America" suggests it will be those nations that understand a re-Asianised Asia will be modern in its own way, and that an American-imposed accounting of friends, allies and enemies will not align to an Asian set of axes.

Can Australia adapt to a changing Asia at a time when its own diplomacy is underfunded, overwhelmed and undervalued? This, for me, is the defining question of the essay. Australia has found itself in a world without assurances. The changeable policy positions of America or China, and their evolving expectations of Australia, leave the future uncertain. Australia will not be ready to meet this moment unless it farewells the America that once was, and welcomes the America that is.

This task can only be achieved with a well-funded Australian diplomatic corps. Diplomacy may not resolve regional tensions, but it remains one of the few policy levers we have that is not likely to damage our relations as post-truth politics adds to competition in Asia. Across a whole range of issues there is a pressing need for Australia to build interest-based coalitions that have enough bargaining power to negotiate the fluctuations of US–China relations. These coalitions are only built one way, through the hard work of diplomacy.

The lack of resources for Australian diplomacy suggests that our leaders do not understand its value. Lawrence finishes his essay with a suggestion that there is hope for Australia as it becomes less Western and more Pacific – that if Australia "enters into a new order", opportunities lie ahead. I would qualify this sentiment – there is only hope and opportunity for Australia if it develops a long-term respect for the interests and aspirations of its geographical region, regardless of how that region might be ordered or labelled.

Thom Dixon is vice president of the Australian Institute of International Affairs branch in New South Wales.

Patrick Lawrence responds

I thank Charles Edel for those things he got right in my essay. "An obsolete understanding of regional dynamics and a nostalgic desire to promote American primacy": a more succinct description of America's problem as it looks across the Pacific I cannot think of. "Wishful thinking born out of 'longing for the once-was, anxiety in the face of change, and an appallingly poor grasp of China's aspirations and intentions'": I cannot be but grateful to Dr Edel for singling out these phrases and ascribing them to wishful thinking. It is precisely the stuff of said nostalgia.

Conveniently enough, Dr Edel also gives *Australian Foreign Affairs* readers an exquisite example of just how these very consequential misapprehensions manage to travel so widely. They are made partly of misjudgements that people of high qualifications ought to be able to avoid, partly of what we may call motivated logic, partly of ideological conformity and partly of distortion. Obfuscatory, cotton-wool language seems always necessary to carry the freight, as Dr Edel's remarks also exemplify. "Actions that have compromised the sovereignty of multiple countries..." Which actions and which countries, please. "... The confrontational foreign policy Beijing has embarked upon..." To what does this refer? This sort of inflated rhetoric simply does not stand up to scrutiny – and is not intended to, so far as I can make out.

This is what you get from the China hawks, unhappily. I will not offend Dr Edel by associating him with the John Birch–like ravings of Mike Pompeo, but he seems to tilt in our thankfully departed secretary of state's direction. In the end it becomes a question of intellectual seriousness.

I am supposed to have argued that "Asia should just get on with the business of accommodating Beijing's interests". Jiminy Cricket! If my essay was about one thing above all others, it was Asians' salutary "re-Asianisation" – their post–Cold War endeavour to define their interests for themselves. Dr Edel cites "the actions [China] has taken to destabilise, coerce and intimidate virtually every single one of its neighbours". Wow, sweeping. I cannot wait to read the list. "Lawrence echoes Beijing's talking points." Oh, please. The veiled suggestion here is too infra dig to engage.

There is more in this line. China "holds out the promise of economic benefit in exchange for political compliance". What under the sun is Dr Edel talking about? Once again, a list of cases would do nicely. Anyone taking the orthodox American position on the China question, as Dr Edel does, ought to (1) stay well clear of this matter of nations that demand political compliance from others and (2) get a good history of America's postwar doings at the western end of the Pacific.

Dr Edel objects to my observation that America is now caught up in a "frenzy of Sinophobia". I do not know how else one would characterise Pompeo's extravagant conjurings of China's countless evils. We've now got the Chinese controlling the weather, tapping Americans' cellular phones from somewhere in the Caribbean, training "super soldiers" to leap tall buildings in a single bound, using some kind of strange ray gun to give American diplomats headaches, and using fun-for-the-family social media applications – TikTok, WeChat – to subvert our republic. Next we will be watching reruns of the Fu Manchu movies.

If readers think I see a twenty-first-century version of the old "yellow peril" in what hawks such as Dr Edel are up to, they read astutely. The point of these incessant fulminations, tinged as they are with primitive xenophobia, should be plain: it is to keep Americans fearful and to justify the Pentagon's presence in the western Pacific – which, as a good map of US military installations will show, is inexcusably immense and provocative. No, as I wrote, East Asians do not want America to retreat to the California coast. But they are not going to sign on for a Cold War II confrontation with the mainland, whether this is offered in the bellicose Pompeo fashion or with the faux sophistication of President Joe Biden's national-security people.

Since my essay was published last October, I have to note, Australia's relations with China have gone straight through the floor. This seems to be the consequence of a long, unfortunately successful campaign waged by hawkish cliques in parliament and government departments, think tanks, the military, the universities and the media. So far as one can make out, these people have been assiduously urged on by Americans such as Dr Edel, whose impeccably hawkish credentials indicate he is well-situated among Sinophobes on both sides of the Pacific.

I had hoped for a better, wiser outcome for Australia, as I made clear in my essay. I had hoped that Australia would quickly see beyond its unbecoming, unconstructive deference to America. Dr Edel insists that Canberra has been thinking for itself all along. And what a splendid irony accompanies this assertion: an American purporting to speak for Australians to say that Australians speak for themselves. I think I understand.

There are some consequential years just out front, as Thom Dixon seems to recognise. Get the China question wrong – choose confrontation over cooperation and coexistence – and America and those who follow it risk damaging (if not disrupting) various longstanding friendships and alliances. Mr Dixon, for whose thoughts and comments I am also grateful, gets it exactly right when he writes of "the contest underway for control of narratives". This is what Pompeo and the various schools of trans-Pacific hawkery wage. And Dixon is right again to say that Australia, finding itself "in a world without assurances", has to make its own way but cannot "unless it farewells the America that once was".

I am certain Australians can get this done and could scarcely cheer them on more vigorously. As Mr Dixon appears to appreciate, it is bound to be a bracing moment to stand between two doors, one ahead to be opened, one behind to be closed. It requires bravery, imagination, the confidence one will find one's way. Strong nations exhibit these qualities. Nations that are merely powerful do not, as a rule, for the simple reason they have no need of these things.

Patrick Lawrence is an American essayist, critic, lecturer and former Asia-based correspondent, and the author of six books.

Subscribe to Australian Foreign Affairs & save up to 28% on the cover price.

Enjoy free home delivery of the print edition and full digital as well as ebook access to the journal via the Australian Foreign Affairs website, iPad, iPhone and Android apps.

Forthcoming issue:
Feeling the Heat
(July 2021)

Never miss an issue. Subscribe and save.

☐ **1 year auto-renewing print and digital subscription** (3 issues) $49.99 within Australia. Outside Australia $79.99*.

☐ **1 year print and digital subscription** (3 issues) $59.99 within Australia. Outside Australia $99.99.

☐ **1 year auto-renewing digital subscription** (3 issues) $29.99.*

☐ **2 year print and digital subscription** (6 issues) $114.99 within Australia.

☐ Tick here to commence subscription with the current issue.

Give an inspired gift. Subscribe a friend.

☐ **1 year print and digital gift subscription** (3 issues) $59.99 within Australia. Outside Australia $99.99.

☐ **1 year digital-only gift subscription** (3 issues) $29.99.

☐ **2 year print and digital gift subscription** (6 issues) $114.99 within Australia.

☐ Tick here to commence subscription with the current issue.

ALL PRICES INCLUDE GST, POSTAGE AND HANDLING.

*Your subscription will automatically renew until you notify us to stop. Prior to the end of your subscription period, we will send you a reminder notice.

Please turn over for subscription order form, or subscribe online at **australianforeignaffairs.com**
Alternatively, call 1800 077 514 or +61 3 9486 0288 or email **subscribe@australianforeignaffairs.com**

Back Issues

ALL PRICES INCLUDE GST,
POSTAGE AND HANDLING.

- [ ] **AFA1** ($15.99)
  The Big Picture

- [ ] **AFA2** ($15.99)
  Trump in Asia

- [ ] **AFA3** ($15.99)
  Australia & Indonesia

- [ ] **AFA4** ($15.99)
  Defending Australia

- [ ] **AFA5** ($15.99)
  Are We Asian Yet?

- [ ] **AFA6** ($15.99)
  Our Sphere of Influence

- [ ] **AFA7** ($15.99)
  China Dependence

- [ ] **AFA8** ($15.99)
  Can We Trust America?

- [ ] **AFA9** ($22.99)
  Spy vs Spy

- [ ] **AFA10** ($22.99)
  Friends, Allies and Enemies

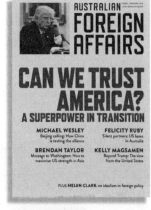

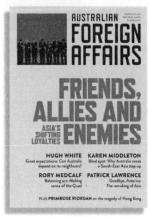

PAYMENT DETAILS I enclose a cheque/money order made out to Schwartz Books Pty Ltd.
Or please debit my credit card (MasterCard, Visa or Amex accepted).

CARD NO.

EXPIRY DATE   /   CCV   AMOUNT $

CARDHOLDER'S NAME

SIGNATURE

NAME

ADDRESS

EMAIL   PHONE

Post or fax this form to: Reply Paid 90094, Carlton VIC 3053 **Freecall:** 1800 077 514 **or** +61 3 9486 0288
Fax: (03) 9011 6106 **Email:** subscribe@australianforeignaffairs.com **Website:** australianforeignaffairs.com
Subscribe online at australianforeignaffairs.com/subscribe (please do not send electronic scans of this form)

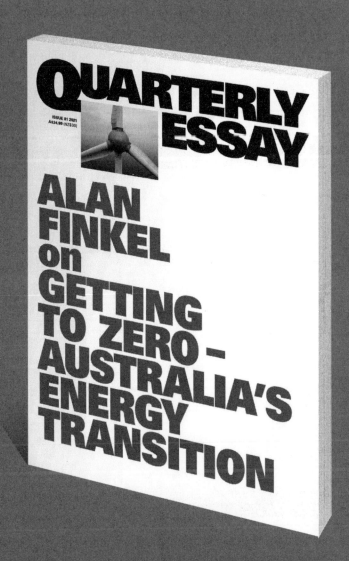

AFA Index

Compiled by Lachlan McIntosh

COVID-19 cases in Australia on 23 March 2020 (lockdown day): 1709
Total cases in Australia as of 1 January 2021: 28,460
Cases in the United States on 23 March 2020: 35,206
Total cases in the United States as of 1 January 2021: 20,190,000

Number of entities on Australia's foreign influence register: 153
Proportion of entities from China: 24 per cent
Proportion of entities from United States: 20 per cent
Number of former Australian public servants on the register: 19

Persons charged under Australia's new foreign interference laws: 1

Australian exports to China in 2018–19: A$153.2 billion
Value of exports currently subject to Chinese sanctions: A$19.4 billion

Proportion of Australians who viewed China positively in 2017: 68 per cent
Proportion who view China positively today: 15 per cent

Aid budget in 2010: A$3.8 billion
Aid budget in 2020: A$4 billion
Aid to the Pacific in 2010: A$1 billion
Aid to the Pacific in 2020: A$1.4 billion

Number of Australian diplomatic posts worldwide: 118
Number of Australian diplomatic posts in the Indo-Pacific: 52
Number of Chinese diplomatic posts worldwide: 276
Number of Chinese diplomatic posts in the Indo-Pacific: 72

Vote for independence in New Caledonia referendum in 2018: 43 per cent
Vote for independence in 2020: 47 per cent
Date of next referendum: 2022

Median age in China in 2010: 35
Median age in China in 2021: 38.4
Median age in the United States in 2010: 37.2
Median age in the United States in 2021: 38.3
Median age in India in 2010: 25.1
Median age in India in 2021: 28.4

FOREIGN POLICY CONCEPTS AND JARGON, EXPLAINED

GREY-ZONE CONFLICT

What is it: Grey-zone conflict or contest has been defined as "acts of coercive statecraft short of war". If war is "the continuation of politics by other means", as Carl von Clausewitz (director, Prussian Kriegsakademie) put it, grey-zone conflict is the continuation of war by other means. The older concepts of "hybrid warfare" and "political warfare" are closely related to the idea.

Where does it happen: Ukraine, the South China Sea and Yemen have all been cited as theatres, where media manipulation, computer hacking, spycraft and propaganda can play a role.

Why does it matter: Some theorists believe grey-zone conflict may replace conventional warfare. According to Robert Muggah (principal, SecDev Group) and John P. Sullivan (former lieutenant, LA County Sheriff's Department), "future conflicts will mostly be waged by drug cartels, mafia groups, gangs, and terrorists".

What can be done: Holding aggressors accountable is challenging. Their methods "do not fit neatly into the current international legal framework" (University of Pennsylvania, Center of Ethics and Rule of Law). Sabotaging infrastructure could be an act of war under *jus ad bellum*, or the right to war, while a cyberattack is in more murky territory: the grey zone.

Collateral damage: In June 2017, US pharmaceutical company Merck & Co. suffered a cyberattack that infected 30,000 of its computers. The source was a Ukrainian office targeted by the GRU, Russia's military intelligence agency. Merck and its insurers are fighting a US$1.3 billion lawsuit over whether this was an act of war.